"MERCILESS REPRESSION"

Human Rights Abuses in Tibet

May 1990

An Asia Watch Report

485 Fifth Avenue
Third Floor
New York, NY 10017
(212) 972-8400
Fax (212) 972-0905

1522 K Street, NW
Suite 910
Washington, DC 20005
(202) 371-6592
Fax (202) 371-0124

ISBN 0-929692-59-4
Library of Congress Card Catalog Number- 90-82361

THE ASIA WATCH COMMITTEE

The Asia Watch Committee was established in 1985 to monitor and promote observance of free expression and other internationally recognized human rights in Asia. The Chairperson of Asia Watch is Jack Greenberg. The Vice Chairperson is Nadine Strossen. Sidney Jones is Executive Director. Mike Jendrzejczyk is Washington Director. Patricia Gossman, Ji Won Park and Robin Munro are Research Associates.

Asia Watch, together with Africa Watch, Americas Watch, Helsinki Watch and Middle East Watch, make up **Human Rights Watch**.

For more information about this and other Asia Watch reports, or concerning Human Rights Watch, please contact:

Human Rights Watch

485 Fifth Avenue
Third Floor
New York, NY 10017
(212) 972-8400
Fax: (212) 972-0905

1522 K Street, NW
Suite 910
Washington, DC 20005
(202) 271-6592
Fax: (202) 371-0124

CONTENTS

INTRODUCTION

In meetings with local officials, Mr. Qiao revealed
Beijing had decided to alter its policy toward Tibet
from lenient to severe...

"The Government of the region must [said Mr.
Qiao] adopt a policy of merciless repression toward
all rebels."

(*UPI*, in *South China Morning Post*,
July 20, 1988)

The above remarks, made by **Qiao Shi,** China's security
chief, in the course of his tour of Tibet in July 1988, show that the
PRC authorities had by then decided upon a course of suppressing
political dissidence in Tibet through the use of unrestricted force
and violence. Events in Tibet over the intervening period have
amply substantiated Qiao's promise of "merciless repression" to
come. A series of initially peaceful protest demonstrations in Lhasa
and elsewhere - notably a small procession on December 10, 1988,
marking International Human Rights Day, and several larger
demonstrations in early March, 1989 - were swiftly and brutally
countered by the Chinese authorities, in a mounting display of
government-inspired violence. Dozens of unarmed Tibetan
demonstrators were killed, and many more have been arbitrarily
arrested in the subsequent security sweeps by Chinese police and
military. In addition, there have been numerous credible reports
of the widespread use of torture against Tibetan political
prisoners, and several known deaths have resulted.

On March 7, 1989, the spiral of repression led finally to
the imposition of martial law in Lhasa, a drastic state of affairs
which, thanks to the authorities' expulsion of foreign observers
from the region, largely removed Tibet from the sphere of direct
international human rights scrutiny. Martial law was officially

1

rescinded on May 1 of this year, but if events in Beijing are any measure, this simply indicates that the mechanism of repression is secure enough as to no longer require a conspicuous military role in suppressing dissent.

Asia Watch has published two previous reports on Tibet: *Human Rights in Tibet* (February 1988), and an update entitled *Evading Scrutiny* (July 1988). Both reports stressed the need for a concerted campaign of international pressure to alleviate what Asia Watch identified as extremely grave human rights violations by the Chinese authorities in Tibet. The Chinese government's response was predictable. Following the release of *Evading Scrutiny*, **Zheng Wanzhen**, press counselor at the Chinese Embassy in Washington, stated bluntly:

> [One suspects] that Asia Watch is not supporting human rights in Tibet, but aiding a handful of former serf masters and their followers and abetting secessionist activities. This of course can only be taken as a crude interference in China's domestic affairs and cannot be tolerated by the Chinese people.[1]

On a number of occasions Asia Watch has pressed a request to send a mission to Tibet to examine human rights conditions there. The Chinese government has consistently refused these requests, arguing that the issue is wholly "an internal Chinese matter" and that any expression of foreign concern or criticism concerning human rights abuses in Tibet is nothing less than a "violation of China's sovereignty."

This report deals with human rights conditions in Tibet in the period since the publication of our last report, *Evading Scrutiny*. However, it is not a simple update, for the scale and

---

[1] *Xinhua* (New China News Agency), July 31, 1988, cited in *Foreign Broadcast Information Service* (hereafter given as *FBIS*), August 1, 1988.

volume of visible human rights abuses have greatly increased since that time. Since September 1987, Tibetan exile sources have reported the occurrence of no less than 30 demonstrations or public displays of political dissent, mostly in and around the Lhasa area, but also in places as far afield as the Tibetan regions of Qinghai and Sichuan. All such manifestations of dissatisfaction with Chinese rule - whether peacefully conducted or otherwise - are viewed by the authorities as constituting "illegal separatist activity", and those who have led or participated in them have been punished with escalating force and severity. "Merciless repression" remains, in Tibet, the order of the day.

In compiling this report we have drawn upon a variety of sources including published articles about Tibet; information from Tibetan exile sources and also data from Tibetans who have just recently fled Tibet; travelers' accounts; interviews with persons who have been in Tibet; and information gathered in the PRC but outside the Tibet Autonomous Region (TAR).[2] The generally consistent nature of the data obtained has enabled us to draw a reasonably accurate profile of the deplorable human rights situation in the region.

Asia Watch is particularly concerned at the grave danger confronting Tibetan human rights monitors, persons who knowingly take upon themselves the potentially fatal risks entailed in working to inform the outside world about continuing human rights violations in Tibet. These people are performing a task that is nothing short of heroic considering the circumstances prevailing in Tibetan areas of the PRC, and we would once more like to recognize their courageous, though necessarily anonymous contributions.

---

[2] Besides those in the TAR, Tibetans live in a number of other autonomous administrative units in the PRC; these are under the jurisdiction of the Chinese provinces of Qinghai, Sichuan, Yunnan and Gansu.

I. POLITICAL REPRESSION

1. Deepening of the Crisis in Tibet: September 1988 to March 1989

Free discussion of political issues in Tibet is highly restricted, and public dissent on Chinese policies in Tibet and on the question of Tibet's status invariably leads to harsh, and sometimes ferocious, punishment. Speeches, writings, and other activities in support of Tibetan independence have occasioned retaliatory measures as cruel as summary execution in the streets. As public demonstrations and other actions in support of Tibetan independence have increased over the past two years and more, repressive measures by the Chinese authorities have become increasingly drastic and routine.

The extent to which demonstrators in Lhasa have remained peaceful and nonviolent is therefore remarkable. Pro-independence demonstrations over the past two years have largely begun non-violently, and the degeneration into violence has generally been precipitated by overt violence on the part of the authorities. For the Chinese authorities, however, the question of whether or not pro-independence demonstrations in Tibet are conducted non-violently appears to be largely irrelevant. Rather, since any activities advocating Tibetan independence are proscribed by Chinese law, their occurrence in any form is held by the authorities to be sufficient cause for the summary and often indiscriminate use of deadly force. Asia Watch takes no position on the status of Tibet; nevertheless we firmly believe Tibetans have a basic human right to express themselves on the issue.

The armed security build-up

The most readily visible indicator of the repressive policy pursued by the PRC authorities in Tibet in recent years is the greatly increased military and police presence in the Lhasa area.

5

In June 1988 the Chinese People's Armed Police (*Renmin Wuzhuang Jingcha*), under the ultimate command of Qiao Shi, created a detachment designed specially to deal "resolute blows at separatists who sabotage the unity of the motherland and the solidarity of nationalities."[3] The unit was established on the second day of Qiao Shi's visit to Tibet on June 15-28, 1988,[4] in the course of which Qiao made the speech from which our opening quotation comes. His remarks received wide circulation in both the foreign and Chinese press[5], and other officials promptly elaborated upon them. In October 1988, for example, Lhasa's vice mayor, **Lamo Rinchen Ozer** (Lha-mo rin-chen 'od-zer, Lamu Renjia Weishe in Chinese), stated:

> Splittists in Tibet who stir up the region's independence and make trouble...must be cracked down on resolutely without mercy....We will deal resolute blows at those who carry out splittist activities and make trouble in Tibet. We seriously warn the small number of splittists that they must

---

[3] *Radio Lhasa*, June 16, 1988; in *FBIS*, June 17, 1988.

[4] "Politburo Member Qiao Shi Inspects Tibet," *Xinhua*, June 30, 1988; in *FBIS*, July 1, 1988.

[5] In addition to the July 20, 1988 *United Press International* report referred to on p.1, above, see: "China Vows to Crack Down in Tibet," *International Herald-Tribune*, July 20, 1988; "A Tibetan Puzzle for Peking," *The Financial Times*, July 23, 1988; "China Gets Ready for Anniversary of Bloody Lhasa Riot," *The Hong Kong Standard*, October 1, 1988; "Tibet Leader Relays Qiao Shi Instructions," *Radio Lhasa*, July 14, 1988, in *FBIS*, same day; "Tibet Commentator Urges Studying Qiao Shi Speech," *Radio Lhasa*, July 14, 1988, in *FBIS* on July 18; and "Tibet CPC Committee Opens Plenary Session," *Radio Lhasa*, October 20, 1988, in *FBIS*, October 21. The actual text of Qiao Shi's speech is not publicly available.

not persist in their stand of opposing the people. We are well prepared. Once a disturbance or riot takes place, we will take severe measures to punish and suppress it. Trouble makers will certainly eat their own bitter fruit.[6]

Numerous foreign press reports subsequently remarked upon the overt presence of Chinese armed forces in and around the Tibetan capital, although their profile was said to be lowered when tour groups were visiting the Tibetan quarter. As the first anniversary of the October 1, 1987 protest demonstrations (the earliest in the recent round of pro-independence activity) neared in late September 1988, the military presence was increased still further, clearly with the aim of intimidating any potential demonstrators. Travelers reported seeing teams of soldiers patrolling the streets on foot and in trucks[7], and independent estimates put the number of troops in the center of Lhasa's Tibetan quarter at 1000 by October 1, China's National Day. Foreign journalists in Lhasa reported that monks who might consider demonstrating had been threatened with execution if they did so, and that an intimidating convoy of shackled Tibetan prisoners had recently been driven through the main street in the Tibetan quarter.[8] Similarly, foreigners in Lhasa were warned not

---

[6] "Lhasa Vice Mayor on Dealing With Disturbances," *Radio Lhasa*, September 30, 1988; in *FBIS*, October 3, 1988.

[7] Patrick Lescot, "Night Curfew for Foreigners Imposed in Tibet," *AFP*, September 27, 1988; in *FBIS*, same day.

[8] David Watts, "Lhasa Parades 'Convicts' to Forestall Unrest," *The Times* (London), September 29, 1988; and *Reuters*, "Monks Threatened With Death," in *The South China Morning Post*, September 14, 1988.

to leave their hotels between 11:30 pm and 6:00 am and not to go
near the Jokhang (the central temple in Lhasa) on October 1.[9]

State coercion in the monasteries

In addition to the armed Chinese presence in the streets of
Lhasa, a similar repressive presence was simultaneously imposed
in monasteries in the vicinity of the Tibetan capital. In late August
and early September 1988, Chinese officials took up residence in
several of the monasteries, clearly in preparation for the coming
first anniversary of the 1987 demonstrations. They held a series of
tough meetings with the resident clergy, reportedly issuing threats
that imprisonment or execution would follow if any
demonstrations were attempted.[10] On September 30, a clash
reportedly took place between officials and monks at the
monastery of **Rato** (Rwa-stod), close to Lhasa, following a heated
exchange between the two sides in which monks began claiming
that Tibet had formerly been an independent country. In the
ensuing violence, as many as twenty monks and neighboring lay
people were said to have been arrested and the monastery was
reportedly closed down. One particularly vocal monk among the
arrested was named as **Tsering Dhondup** (Tshe-ring
Don-grub).[11]   Tibetan exile sources have reported that several
of the monks arrested were severely beaten before and during
interrogation.

---

[9] Patrick Lescot, "Police Presence Discourages Tibet
Demonstrations," *AFP* October 3, 1988, in *FBIS*, October 4, 1988;
and David Watts, "Lhasa Parades 'Convicts' to Forestall Unrest,"
The Times (London), September 29, 1988.

[10] David Watts, "Lhasa Parades 'Convicts' to Forestall Unrest,"
The Times, September 29, 1988.

[11] Daniel Southerland, "Tibetan Monks Clash With Police,"
The Washington Post, November 1, 1988.

The December 10 suppression

On December 10, Chinese police opened fire on a group of demonstrators in Tibet, killing at least two and wounding many others, as dozens marched beneath the outlawed Tibetan flag in Lhasa to commemorate the 40th anniversary of the adoption of the Universal Declaration of Human Rights. Although the nationally televised evening news in China said that police fired after demonstrators threw bottles and stones at them, eyewitnesses reported that police shot without warning.[12]

International coverage noted that the lead monk in the demonstration, **Gyalpo** (Rgyal-po)[13], was shot at almost point-blank range as he marched along peacefully.[14] In addition, a Dutch woman received a bullet-wound in the arm; the authorities, however, claimed her presence in Lhasa was suspicious and later

---

[12] *News From Asia Watch*, "Chinese Police Shoot Tibetan Demonstrators During Human Rights Day Demonstration," December 16, 1988.

[13] Also known as: Ngawang Kunga (Ngag-dbang kun-dga').

[14] See James L. Tyson, "Peking Takes More Violent Tack in Dealing With Tibetan Rebels," *Christian Science Monitor*, December 12, 1988; Tim Luard, "Tibetans Shot As They Join China's First 'Rights Day,'" *Daily Telegraph*, December 12, 1988; Danny Gittings, "Tibetans Killed By China Police," *The Guardian*, December 12, 1988; Nicholas D. Kristof, "Two Are Said to Die in Tibet Protests," *The New York Times*, December 11, 1988; Daniel Southerland, "Police Shoot at Protesters in Tibet," *The Washington Post*, December 11, 1988; "Chinese Police Kill Three In Lhasa Violence," *The South China Morning Post*, December 11, 1988; and "18 died In December Demonstration: Chinese Report," *Tibetan Review*, February, 1989.

accused her of having been sent into Tibet with instructions to organize a riot.[15]

In the wake of the Human Rights Day protest, Tibetan officials in the TAR broadcast wrathful condemnations of those advocating Tibet's independence. According to one official: "It is necessary to punish severely a small number of splittists according to the law, and no appeasement should be applied to them."[16] The authoritative magazine *Liaowang* (Outlook) summarized as follows the stern view from Beijing:

> Tibet is an inalienable part of Chinese territory. Any splittist action is not allowed by state law. Independence, semi-independence, or independence in a disguised form will never be tolerated...
>
> The riots in Lhasa were engineered and instigated by a handful of splittist elements inside and outside Tibet. They tried to split Tibet from the big family of the motherland. This will never be allowed by law, or tolerated by the Tibetan people.[17]

The armed Chinese presence once again visibly increased, both in the streets of Lhasa and in the local monasteries. Military street patrols were instituted, and nine busloads of People's Armed Police personnel were driven to the monasteries of **Sera** (Se-ra) and **Drepung** ('Bras-spungs), where several monks were then

---

[15] "Comment on Martial Law," *Xinhua* March 21, 1989; in FBIS, March 22.

[16] "Tibetan Patriots Stress National Unity," *Radio Lhasa*, December 13, 1988; in *FBIS*, December 14, 1988.

[17] "*Liaowang* Discusses Tibetan Affairs," in *FBIS*, December 20, 1988; from *Liaowang* (Overseas Edition), December 19, 1988.

arrested.[18] This armed presence was, of course, additional to the large numbers of non-uniformed Chinese security personnel whose usual presence in the streets of the Tibetan quarter we noted in *Human Rights in Tibet*. Once Chinese control had been fully reestablished, much of the armed presence was withdrawn from the Tibetan quarter, but it remained in place elsewhere in the capital. Non-uniformed police contingents and the occasional truckload of troops continued to make sweeps through the area.[19]

Just prior to the military crackdown and imposition of martial law in Lhasa in March 1989, senior party officials were quoted by Reuters as saying that China must "maintain a high degree of vigilance and wage a resolute struggle against destructive separatist activities" and that China would "severely crack down" on separatists.[20] Echoing the point, **Ismail Amat**, a senior member of China's State Nationalities Affairs Commission stressed the need to "resolutely fight against any separatist activity."[21] The foreign press reported that Tibetans had been

[18] Danny Gittings, "Chinese get tough with protesters," *The Guardian*, December 13, 1988.

[19] David Holley, "Tibet's Hunger to Be Free Symbolized by Dalai Lama," *Los Angeles Times*, January 21, 1989.

[20] "China Warns Restless Minorities," *The Washington Times*, February 22, 1989.

[21] "Nationalities Minister Criticizes Separatism," *Renmin Ribao* (People's Daily), February 22, 1989; in *FBIS*, February 28, 1989.

warned by the authorities that they would risk being shot should they venture to demonstrate.[22]

---

[22] See "*AFP* Views 'Harder Line' on Tibetan Protesters," *FBIS*, December 12, 1988 (on report from Patrick Lescot of *AFP*, same day); and Danny Gittings, "Chinese Get Tough With Protesters," *The Guardian*, December 13, 1988.

2. The March 1989 Demonstrations and the Period of Martial Law in Lhasa

The most serious violence in the recent series of protests in Tibet occurred during the large-scale demonstrations of March 5-7, 1989, events which led directly to the imposition of martial law in the area in and around Lhasa. These demonstrations were undoubtedly intended to commemorate the demonstration held at the end of the Great Prayer, or Monlam Chenmo (Smon-lam chen-mo) Festival a year earlier which had degenerated into violent confrontation between protesters and security personnel, resulting in the death of a member of the armed security forces.[23]

According to Tibetan exile sources, the events that led directly to the imposition of martial law began with a peaceful protest by Tibetans near the **Jokhang**, the main temple in Lhasa, around noon on March 5, 1989. A small procession of less than 40 individuals circled the temple twice and then found itself facing armed security personnel who had taken up positions on the roof of the area's police station. The police are said to have thrown bottles at the protesters, who responded with rocks. The police then began shooting at the demonstrators. Shortly before 12:30 pm tear gas was fired, and several minutes later automatic rifles were fired by the police. For two hours afterwards, a series of running confrontations between demonstrators and security forces took place. Just before 2:30, automatic weapons were once more fired. At 2:30 a larger group of Tibetans (up to 1000) tried to circle the Jokhang again, and were dispersed with tear gas. The people then regrouped on **Dekyi Road East** (Bde-skyid shar lam, also referred to as Beijing Road), the road running from the

---

[23] Four young Tibetans were arrested and later tried and convicted on account of this killing. See below, p.41, for details of the criminal proceedings against the four. A full account of the events of March 5, 1988 is given in *Evading Scrutiny*, pp.17-23.

Tibetan quarter down to the **Potala Palace**, and at 3:30 a group of armed police personnel charged the crowd, launching tear gas and firing automatic weapons. As the Tibetans fell back, attacks began against Chinese shops along the road. By the end of the day, between 20 and 25 shops had been gutted and their contents taken out and burned. Several further periods of sustained automatic weapons fire ensued before nightfall.

On March 6, crowds began gathering on Dekyi Road East late in the morning, harassing cyclists, throwing stones and burning bicycles and the contents of shops (presumably owned by Chinese migrants). By mid-afternoon the government tax office was burned and several shops in the **Barkor** (Bar-skor) area, the area around the road circling the Jokhang, were gutted. Police began to fire at the crowds from a rooftop, and in the early evening, they began to advance up Dekyi Road East against the Tibetans. They vacated the area for an hour, between 7:30 and 8:30 in the evening, but on their return they fired tear gas canisters and automatic weapons at Tibetans who had returned to the streets in their absence. Automatic weapons fire continued sporadically into the night.

By March 7, the violence had subsided considerably, but small crowds still came out into the streets and periodic firing was heard. Only after dark did Chinese forces move into the area in large numbers. Perhaps 1000 People's Armed Police personnel together with People's Liberation Army (PLA) forces took up positions in the Tibetan quarter and began going to Tibetan homes. In the early hours of the morning, Public Security Bureau personnel visited the small number of foreign tourists in Lhasa and announced that they were going to be expelled from Lhasa and that martial law was to be imposed in the area.[24] Reached by telephone, foreign tourists in the city were able to describe

_____

[24] This account is drawn from a compilation of notes made by foreign tourists in Lhasa and published as "Eyewitness Account of the March Riots," *Tibetan Review*, April, 1989, pp. 4-5.

mass arrests and a Tibetan death toll that was initially estimated to have reached perhaps 60, with 100 wounded.

There were apparently less than 100 tourists in Tibet during the events just described, the number of tourists having dropped off sharply following the travel restrictions imposed after the protests of late 1987. These travelers were mostly confined to their hotels prior to expulsion, seemingly in order to sever further contact between them and Tibetans, and so sealing off a potentially embarrassing source of information on the unfolding repression in Lhasa. A British journalist who had managed to get to Lhasa was detained, interrogated and threatened at gun point, before he and a colleague were ordered out of Tibet. Also, a Swiss national who had taken pictures of the riots reported having been beaten at gun point.[25] According to one of the tourists interviewed by telephone, at least 100 soldiers had taken up positions on the street where his hotel was located (probably Dekyi Road East), with witnesses adding that at least 2000 troops had taken up positions in Tibet on the evening of March 7. It was also clear that the shops and restaurants that had been the target of Tibetan attacks were Chinese enterprises.[26]

The Chinese authorities' hostility toward foreign observers in the wake of the violent unrest of early March, 1989, did not prevent them from trying to impart a tone of "foreign detachment" to their own dispatches, in attempts to add credibility to their version of events. An official Chinese news dispatch put out in Hong Kong, for example, quoted a "tourist who refused to reveal his identity" as stating that the riot, like that of the year before, had been the work of a small number of monks and nuns, and

---

[25] "Correspondent Threatened," *FBIS*, March 10, 1989 (article from the *South China Morning Post*); and "Tibetans' Houses Raided by Chinese Troops, *The New York Times*, March 9, 1989.

[26] Patrick Lescot, "'Mass Arrests' Carried Out," *AFP*, March 8, 1989; in *FBIS*, same day.

that the rioters had carried pistols and a machine gun.[27]
Another Chinese dispatch quoted an American national teaching
in Lhasa as declaring that the Chinese government had made "a
wise and timely" move in deciding to impose martial law in the
Lhasa area.[28]

Official Chinese accounts of the demonstrations and riots
in Lhasa all stressed the destruction that had occurred, the
violence of the demonstrators, and their alleged possession of
weapons and foreign linkages to the riots. The Chinese media
made repeated references to "beating, smashing, looting, and
burning," in characterizing the disturbances.[29] (This is the same
charge that was later used against arrested pro-democracy
demonstrators throughout China in the nationwide repression that
followed the June 4, 1989 massacre in Beijing.) In addition to the
attacks on Chinese-owned and operated shops and businesses, and
on Chinese government offices, attention was drawn to the general
disruption of schooling and the smashing of windows in one
school,[30] and to similar destruction at a hospital.[31]

---

[27] "Eyewitness Cited on 'Riots'," *Zhongguo Tongxun She*, March
6, 1989; in *FBIS*, same day.

[28] "American Professor Praises Martial Law," *Xinhua*, March 9,
1989; in *FBIS*, March 10.

[29] See various reports grouped under the headings: "Further
Reportage on Tibetan Riots, Situation," *FBIS*, March 7, 1989;
"Further Reportage on Tibetan Riots, Aftermath," *FBIS*, March 8,
1989; and "Further Reportage, Commentary on Tibetan Riots,"
FBIS, March 9, 1989.

[30] "Lhasa Schools Affected," *Radio Lhasa*, March 7, 1989, in
FBIS, same day; "Peace 'Gradually Returns'," from *Zhongguo Xinwen
She*, March 14, 1989, in *FBIS*, March 15, 1989; "Primary School
Resumes Classes," *Xinhua*, March 20, 1989, in *FBIS*, March 21,
1989; and "Lhasa: From Riots to Martial Law," *Beijing Review*,

Furthermore, Chinese reports maintained that many Tibetans had carried and used guns during the violence. They stated that the demonstrators had commandeered a building along Dekyi Road East, using it as a sniper's nest from which they had fired on police, security personnel and passersby.[32] Ultimately the Chinese government adopted the position that separatist groups outside the country had colluded with travelers who entered Tibet as tourists in smuggling arms into Tibet in preparation for the riots.[33]

The charge that Tibetans had used guns - ostensibly one reason for the authorities' imposition of martial law[34] - is not new. Following the degeneration into violence of the demonstrations in the fall of 1987, the Chinese government similarly accused participants of having used guns, although foreigners on the scene maintained that no Tibetans had been

---

March 27-April 2, 1989.

[31] "Account of 5, 6 March Riots," *Xinhua*, March 7, 1989; in *FBIS*, March 8, 1989.

[32] Ibid.

[33] "Commentator on Human Rights," *Xinhua*, March 8, 1989, in *FBIS*, March 9, 1989; and "Lhasa: From Riots to Martial Law," *Beijing Review*, March 27-April 2, 1989. Declared one report: "Following the opening of Tibet to the outside world, it is logical that the evildoers will smuggle weapons to the region to hatch their sinister plot." ("Necessity of Martial Law Viewed," *Ta Kung Pao*, March 8, 1989; in *FBIS*, same day.)

[34] "Commentary on 'Tibetan Independence'," *Zhongguo Tongxun She*, March 8, 1989; in *FBIS*, March 9, 1989. See also "Lhasa: From Riots to Martial Law," *Beijing Review*, March 27-April 2, 1989.

seen with guns.[35] Similarly, foreigners present in Lhasa in March 1989 emphatically stated that no Tibetans were seen carrying or using guns. A foreign reporter added that, as far as he could observe, none of the Tibetans had carried any weapons other than the traditional knives that many of them usually carry. He expressed skepticism concerning Chinese reports that arms had been smuggled into Tibet, and emphasized that the original demonstration had degenerated into violence as a result of the way the authorities had chosen to handle it. He was quoted as saying:

> It did not start off as a violent demonstration and the police could have let it bubble on that way....Violence was not necessary. The demonstrators did not intend to beat up Chinese, but by meeting it (the demonstration) with force, the police precipitated the action.[36]

A small group of travelers speaking in Hong Kong, after having been expelled from Tibet, maintained that the police at first had moved into the Tibetan quarter in a fairly disorderly manner and that "they were just spraying gunfire with no particular target."[37] One person from the group again denied allegations that the Tibetans had had guns and had fired on Chinese, while a Thai businessman described Chinese security

---

[35] See *Human Rights in Tibet* (Asia Watch) p.59.

[36] "Chinese Blamed for Violence," *The South China Morning Post*, March 11, 1989; in *FBIS*, March 13.

[37] "Police Reportedly in 'Disarray,'" *AFP*, March 13, 1989; in *FBIS*, same day.

forces as having "walked up, knelt and fired at unarmed people."[38] Similarly, a group of 35 tourists who had witnessed the events drew up a collective statement in which they blamed the authorities in Lhasa for precipitating the violence:

> While the Tibetan demonstrators became violent and destructive in expressing their anger and frustration, we feel that the magnitude and bloodiness of the crisis has been caused by the incompetence of the authorities.... Shootings by the authorities have been excessive, unpredictable, indiscriminate, and there have on occasion been atrocities.[39]

The authorities attempted to counter such charges by defensively reiterating the official PRC version of pre-1949 Tibetan social realities and by stressing the violent nature of the recent clashes in Lhasa:

> [Foreigners] have mentioned nothing about the feudal system of serfdom implemented in Tibet, the miserable life that a million serfs were leading and the past forces of aggression riding roughshod in Tibet in the past. Here these gentlemen seem to show no concern about the issue of "human rights"...
>
> Flames raged along the streets and a large number of Tibetan houses and stores were destroyed within the short period since March 5. Everywhere a scene

---

[38] "Authorities 'Aware' of Riots," *The South China Morning Post*, March 10, 1989; in *FBIS*, same day.

[39] "'Excessive Action' Claimed by Tourists,"*AFP*, March 9, 1989; in *FBIS*, same day.

of devastation meets the eye. Is this the peaceful demonstration or parade mentioned by some foreign gentlemen?[40]

At the end of March the mayor of Lhasa, speaking in Beijing, replied to a query from the *Washington Post* correspondent in the Chinese capital on the firearms question, stating that "A small number of firearms have been confiscated and we are in the process of finding their sources....We are also sure who organized these riots..." According to a Chinese report on the press conference, the mayor added: "The truth will be made known in due time since it is not fit to show the evidence today."[41]

The martial law regulations ordered on March 7 and 8 were harsh and graphically illustrate the extent to which the authorities had become willing to publicly impose policies in Tibet that were in clear violation of basic human rights, regardless of international concern. The regulations banned assemblies and demonstrations, restricted movement in the martial law area and ordered unauthorized foreigners out. In addition, security forces were ordered to take necessary measures to halt a variety of acts, including any instigation of separatism, and to detain those involved on the spot. Furthermore, those who had sheltered persons involved in the riots were told to surrender and severe punishment was ordered for anyone retaliating against informers.

---

[40] "Tibetan Riots Reviewed; Situation Improving," in *FBIS*, April 25, 1989, from *Liaowang* (Overseas Edition), March 20, 1989. Again, the article stressed: "What attracts particular attention and makes people uneasy is the fact that the rioters had used weapons during the incident and that weapons had been smuggled into China from abroad."

[41] "Evidence Cited of Rioters Fighting," *Xinhua*, March 31, 1989; in *FBIS*, same day.

The wave of arrests

In the wholesale repression that followed the issuance of these martial law regulations, large-scale arrests of Tibetans suspected of involvement in separatist actions of any sort were successively carried out. They began even before the departure of foreign travelers, as perhaps more than 2000 soldiers proceeded to take up positions in Lhasa,[42] and it is clear that arrests multiplied once the foreign travelers and journalists had all left.[43] Just prior to the expulsion of these foreigners from Lhasa, an American tourist told a reporter:

> The Tibetans are frightened to death at what's going to happen when the foreigners go....Many times in the past week I've been with Tibetans who have been absolutely beside themselves in tears, just terrified at what's going to happen..."[44]

According to another report, Tibetans told departing Western travelers: "We are finished. We are finished....Once you are gone, they will take us away."[45]

In the immediate aftermath of the mass arrests of March 1989, State Council spokesman **Yuan Mu** was still willing to state to reporters, with regard to political imprisonment in the PRC as a whole: "China punishes criminals according to the law. There

---

[42] "'Mass Arrests' Carried Out," *AFP*, March 8, 1989; in *FBIS*, same day.

[43] "More Arrests Reported," *AFP*, March 10, 1989; in *FBIS*, same day.

[44] "Departure of Foreigners Raise Fears," *AFP*, March 9, 1989; in *FBIS*, same day.

[45] "Further on Denial," *The Hongkong Standard*, March 10, 1989; in *FBIS*, March 13.

are no political prisoners in China. Therefore the question of releasing political prisoners does not exist."[46] As *Martial Law Decree No. 2* made clear, however, merely advocating ("instigating") Tibetan independence now constituted sufficient grounds for imprisonment in Tibet - regardless of whether or not the accused had participated in acts of violence. According to one unconfirmed report, Tibetan sources in Lhasa estimated that approximately 1000 Tibetans were arrested immediately after the imposition of martial law.[47]

At the end of March, Lhasa's mayor stated that over 300 Tibetans had thus far been detained in connection with the demonstration.[48] Tibetan exile sources placed the number of arrests by this time as possibly exceeding 10,000,[49] while a report from Hong Kong stated that of the more than 360 Tibetans believed to have been arrested, there were said to be 1760 Tibetan party members and government officials.[50] Tibetan exiles also maintained that Tibetan participants in earlier demonstrations who had already been released were being rearrested. A reporter

---

[46] "Video Report on Briefing," from Beijing Television, March 14, 1989, in *FBIS*, March 15.

[47] "Further on Denial," *The Hongkong Standard*, March 10, 1989.

[48] Daniel Southerland, "300 Tibetans Said Arrested After Rioting," *The Washington Post*, April 1, 1989; "Tibet Officials Say 300 Demonstrators Are Being Detained," *The New York Times*, April 1, 1989; and "Lhasa Mayor on Policies Toward Tibet," *Xinhua*, March 31, 1989, in *FBIS*, same day.

[49] Barbara Crossette, "Dalai Lama Sees a Culture Endangered," *The New York Times*, March 22, 1989.

[50] "Tibetan Toll," *The Far Eastern Economic Review*, April 13, 1989.

who visited Lhasa in July was told by Tibetan monks that 500 other monks had been imprisoned for participation in past disturbances.[51] A British journalist who visited Lhasa in October was told by **Wang Naiwen**, a Public Security Bureau spokesman, that more than 400 Tibetans had been arrested since March.

Both official and unofficial sources put the total number of Tibetans in Lhasa's prisons at more than 1000. Wang Naiwen also indicated that about 83 people had received three-year labor camp sentences without having been tried, while 320 had been released from detention.[52] An American reporter was told in December by a Tibetan monk that while 3000 people had been arrested initially and 70 executed, the authorities were presently holding 1000 people as a result of the March protests.[53] While none of these figures can be verified by Asia Watch, we are certain that at least several hundred Tibetans have been arrested since the violence of March 1989. Some of the detained Tibetans have been accused by the Chinese authorities of being agents of the Dalai Lama and the Tibetan exile authorities.[54] Reports that Tibetans

---

[51] Arthur Kent, "Rule by Kalashnikov," *The Observer*, July 23, 1989.

[52] Guy Dinmore, "China Denies Allegations of Prison Beatings, Torture in Tibet," *Reuters*, October 22, 1989.

[53] Lewis M. Simons, "A Populace Seethes," *The Boston Globe*, December 7, 1989.

[54] Chinese officials even implicated Japanese citizens and organizations in the supposed conspiracy: "We confirmed that [the Tibetan exile authorities] had shipped many weapons into Tibet; and that they had sent in some people who had undergone special training in Japan. These people were not trained by the Japanese government, of course, but by different kinds of organizations that paid for the training. Soon after we learned this, we sent a

who had earlier been released were rearrested after the March riots are also difficult to verify, but are certainly plausible, given the overall severity of the crackdown.

As martial law came into force, at midnight on March 7, Western tourists described Tibetans screaming in the night as they were being hauled away by the security forces.

> These were women's voices....The truck kept coming back. They would pick up a couple of people, drive off with a half dozen militia holding them down, then come back.... [Elsewhere] they were just collaring people on the street and stuffing them into jeeps.[55]

Chinese accounts of the arrests had, of course, a wholly different tone. According to some, Tibetans who had participated in the protests were voluntarily turning themselves in to the

---

message to the Dalai Lama and requested that he stop doing this if he really wanted to improve relations with us. Aware of our strict control, the Dalai then turned to foreign tourists to infiltrate Tibet through various channels, showing no sincerity in attempting to improve relations with us." ("Yan Mingfu Opposes Dalai Lama Separatist Trends," *Zhongguo Xinwen She*, March 21, 1989; in *FBIS*, March 22.) These charges were denied by Tibetan exile authorities. See for example: "Outside Instigation Denied," *The South China Morning Post*, March 13, 1989, in *FBIS*, same day; and "Further on Denial," *The Hongkong Standard*, March 10, 1989, in *FBIS*, March 13.

[55] Kathy Wilhelm, "Screams as troops grab Tibet rebels," *The Herald* (Australia), March 9. 1989.

authorities and then naming other participants.[56] One Chinese reporter who made the rounds of Lhasa in the company of the police described as follows the start of the mass arrests:

> At 00:00 on 8 March, when martial law went into force, I went to the Bajiao Street [i.e., Barkor] police station. In cooperation with the public security personnel and armed police, the detachment to search and arrest rioters set out in orderly formation. I followed the detachment to a small lane on the southwest of Bajiao Street. The detachment stopped in front of an old building in Punu Road and knocked at one of the doors. When a male rioter realized that he was in trouble he burst into tears and begged for mercy. Another rioter in the neighborhood saw the public security personnel presenting the arrest warrant. He remained in his quilt pretending to be ignorant. Later he pretended to be calm. His wife pushed him, saying: "Put on your clothes. Why didn't you listen to me. I told you not to go."[57]

A subsequent report on the more than 300 Tibetans whose arrests have been acknowledged by the Chinese authorities described the detainees as being:

> [T]rouble-makers, some of them members of "underground reactionary organizations"....Police have seized [from them] a large number of books,

---

[56] "Rioters Surrender to Police," *Renmin Ribao*, March 10, 1989, in *FBIS*, same day; and "Streets Remain Quiet," *Renmin Ribao*, March 11, 1989, in *FBIS*, March 13.

[57] "Martial Law Results Viewed," *Renmin Ribao*, March 9, 1989; in *FBIS*, March 10.

magazines, leaflets and radio cassettes containing "reactionary propaganda." Unlawful firearms and ammunition, as well as explosives were also captured...[58]

It has been reliably reported that Tibetans arrested during the demonstrations were subjected to beatings,[59] a charge that is fully consistent with reports of police treatment of detainees following previous demonstrations. Subsequently, graphic proof of vicious police beatings of Tibetan detainees has appeared in the form of a videotape that was smuggled out of Tibet and shown on US television. The videotape of the suppression of the March 1988 demonstration that was shown, in part, on the US television program "20/20" in the spring of 1989, contained clear scenes of detained monks being severely beaten by Chinese security forces. Asia Watch is particularly concerned, however, about reports of the continued use of torture against those arrested in the aftermath of the March 1989 violence. The use of torture against political prisoners in Tibet predates the imposition of martial law and the chain of political protests that began in 1987, and Asia Watch believes that the abuse is still systematically perpetrated in Tibetan prisons today. (A number of such cases, dating from both before and after the imposition of martial law, are presented in Chapter 5.)

In the period since the implementation of martial law in Tibet, information about the situation there has been harder to obtain. Martial law simply served to solidify and intensify the air of repression that has consistently been an obstacle to free political discourse and protest. At present it appears that the ending of

---

[58] "Lhasa Returning to Normal," *Xinhua*, April 1, 1989; in *FBIS*, April 3.

[59] "Police Reportedly Roundup Rioters," *AFP*, March 6, 1989; in *FBIS*, same day.

martial law on May 1 has not altered this basic fact of political life in Tibet.

Under martial law the army has had the right to stop and search people and vehicles at will. In addition, a British correspondent visiting Lhasa in October reported it was virtually impossibile to have any open conversations with Tibetans, since he was constantly accompanied by a government official.[60] The air of suspicion and surveillance was further reinforced by government directives, such as a broadcast on Lhasa radio in November 1989, which declared:

> [The city's cadres should] take the lead in carrying out political, ideological, propaganda, and educational work among the masses as well as among their relatives and family members, take a firm stand in the struggle against separatism, and expose and inform against separatists and other serious criminal offenders.[61]

The creation, by such intimidatory means, of an atmosphere of fear of being informed against (perhaps even by one's own family members) constitutes a serious act of harassment by the authorities. In Asia Watch's view this impinges on and subverts the basic human right to free expression. Such tactics do not appear to have eliminated the sentiments against which they are directed. When news reached Lhasa in October that the Dalai Lama had been awarded the Nobel Peace Prize, for example, informal celebration parties were reportedly held. The authorities are said to have arrested and interrogated over 200 Tibetans, but

---

[60] Guy Dinmore, "No End to Martial Law in Lhasa in Sight," *Reuters*, October 10, 1989.

[61] "Tibet Issues Screening, Investigation Circular," *Radio Lhasa*, November 25, 1989; in *FBIS*, December 13.

that did not deter other Tibetans from holding small scale independence demonstrations that predictably resulted in further arrests.[62] Clear signs of anti-Chinese feeling were observed by some of the few visitors who were able to travel to Lhasa as recently as December 1989.[63]

---

[62] "New Crackdown Follows Celebrations in Lhasa," *The Washington Post*, December 21, 1989; and John Gittings, "Tibetan Nuns Defy the Might of China," *The Guardian*, November 8, 1989.

[63] Lewis M. Simons, "A Populace Seethes," *The Boston Globe*, December 7, 1989.

3. Political Imprisonment in Tibet

Political imprisonment under harsh conditions is the principal means by which the authority of China has been brought to bear upon dissenting Tibetans since Deng Xiaoping came to power. This practice is in clear violation of the internationally recognized right to freedom of political belief and to the peaceful expression of such beliefs. Asia Watch's first report on Tibet, completed in early 1988 shortly after the first in the recent round of demonstrations in the region, was unequivocal in describing and condemning the Chinese authorities' extensive use of political imprisonment prior to those protests.

The decreased visibility of political imprisonment and torture since the imposition of martial law in March 1989 should on no account be taken as indicating any decrease in the incidence of such abuses now. To the contrary, all available evidence points to a further deterioration in the human rights situation in these two key respects. While China's press restrictions have seriously hampered foreign coverage of events in Tibet, concerned observers have still been able to read and hear detailed press, radio and television accounts of imprisonment and torture there, and even (as mentioned above) to view video footage of Chinese security personnel beating up helpless Tibetan detainees.

The releases of mid- to late-1988

The wave of political arrests that accompanied the start of martial law in Lhasa was preceded by a brief period of respite for Tibetan pro-independence activists. In July 1988, the Chinese media announced the release of 52 monks and nuns who had been imprisoned following the protest demonstrations of the previous

March.[64] Over the following months, large numbers of Tibetans imprisoned for their participation in those and earlier demonstrations were also released from prisons in and around Lhasa. These releases, seemingly at odds with the hardline policy enunciated by Qiao Shi some months earlier, may be attributable to the following factors. The first is an apparent belief on the part of the authorities that their repressive measures against the Tibetan independence movement had already, by mid-1988, been sufficiently effective in eradicating dissent.[65] The second factor seems to have been a dawning awareness in government circles of the adverse impact that the steadily mounting expressions of international concern over human rights violations in Tibet were starting to have on China's international image and on its relations with other countries.

In August 1988, the Chinese government allowed a delegation of three US senators into Tibet led by **Sen. Patrick Leahy** of Vermont, and accompanied by a small group of Western reporters.[66] The authorities continued to maintain large police

---

[64] See: "Lamas Detained in March During Riots Released," *Xinhua*, July 11, 1988, in *FBIS*, July 12; "Tibet Releases 52 Monks," *Radio Lhasa*, July 12, 1988, in *FBIS*, July 13; and "Lama Rioters Released in Lhasa," *Beijing Review*, July 25-31, 1988.

[65] This (if true) recalls a similar miscalculation on the part of the authorities when delegations from the Dalai Lama's "Government-in-Exile" were allowed to visit Tibet for a brief period beginning in 1979; these visits likewise precipitated unforeseen demonstrations of affection for the delegates and displays of antipathy toward the Chinese authorities.

[66] According to the report of one of these journalists, Tibetans released from prison expressed the belief that new sensitivity on the part of the authorities was what had brought about their releases; see Donald Southerland, "Tibetan Tells Of Torture," *The Washington Post*, September 6, 1988.

and security deployments throughout Lhasa.[67] The earlier report that 52 monks and nuns had been released in July was corroborated by journalists in Leahy's party, and in interviews with some of the former detainees they learned about conditions of incarceration in Tibet and also of the torture to which some of them had been subjected.[68] No list of names of those released was obtained, let alone a breakdown of the cases by dates of arrest or charge that might have revealed the overall course of political imprisonment in Tibet since the inception of the current protest movement in late 1987.

On October 27, 1988, Asia Watch requested from **Han Xu**, then the Chinese ambassador to the US, information concerning all political prisoners who had been or were being released, and on those still being held. On December 2, 1988, shortly before the violent supression of the Human Rights Day demonstration in Lhasa, an Asia Watch representative met with the first secretary in the Chinese Embassy's press office, **Wu Zurong**. The first secretary read out a prepared statement to the effect that several hundred prisoners had recently been released from prison in Tibet. The statement added that most of those arrested since the major demonstrations in late 1987 and March 1988 had: "...been released or dealt with leniently, and only 22 people now remain in custody." The statement ignored Asia Watch's request for a list of persons imprisoned in Tibet for politically motivated offenses.

---

[67] Pierre-Antoine Donnet, "Continuing Tibetan Resistance to Police Reported," *AFP*, December 6, 1988; in *FBIS*, same day.

[68] See Donald Southerland, "Tibetan Tells Of Torture," *The Washington Post*, September 6, 1988. The report states that those who were not released were "considered to be leaders of the Tibetan independence movement, persons who participated in more than one demonstration, or persons who are believed to come from families or groups known to be anti-Chinese."

In response to our renewed request for permission to directly examine human rights conditions in Tibet, Wu stated:

> We are unable to make accommodation for those visitors who wish to visit China for investigating the human rights situation in Tibet, for problems in Tibet are internal affairs of China which brook no foreign interference.

Asia Watch believes that the number of Tibetans who remained in prison for political offenses during this period was considerably higher than 22. The Chinese Embassy statement refers only to prisoners arrested in late 1987 and March 1988, while Asia Watch has described in its earlier reports a systematic policy of political imprisonment that predated the 1987 demonstrations.

Political Imprisonment Beyond the Lhasa Region:

Kumbum

Tibetans are reliably reported to have been arrested after demonstrations in places other than Lhasa. The cases of two Tibetan prisoners from **Kumbum** (Sku-'bum, or *Taersi* in Chinese) are illustrative. A large, well-known Tibetan monastery in one of the Tibetan areas of Qinghai province, Kumbum is located near the northeast edge of the Tibetan Plateau, less than one hour's drive from the provincial capital of Xining. Following the brutal suppression of the March 1988 demonstrations in Lhasa, Tibetan exile sources reported that demonstrations protesting the authorities' use of violence in Lhasa had erupted spontaneously in several places in Tibetan areas in the eastern portion of the Tibetan Plateau, outside the boundaries of the TAR, and that arrests had followed. Asia Watch has independently learned that a small group of monks held a modest protest march through the grounds of Kumbum at this time, and that shortly thereafter security personnel raided the monastery at night, under cover of darkness, and arrested several participants.

These included two monks named **Yeshe Sangpo** (Ye-shes bzang-po), 27, arrested at Kumbum, and **Lobsang Tsultrim** (Blo-bzang tshul-khrims), 26, who was captured en route while attempting to escape to Nepal. The places of imprisonment of these two monks are not known,[69] and it should be stressed that neither of their names appear on any of the various lists of Tibetan political prisoners compiled by Tibetan exile sources. For the most part, these lists (which are far from complete) provide details only of prisoners held in and around Lhasa, and Asia Watch believes that many other Tibetans whose cases resemble those of Yeshe Sangpo and Lobsang Tsultrim are currently imprisoned in Tibetan areas of the PRC lying beyond the boundaries of the TAR.

Political imprisonment since martial law

In March 1989, following the three days of violent protest demonstrations that led to the imposition of martial law in Lhasa, arrests of Tibetan political dissidents once again increased

---

[69] We found a general reluctance to speak about these events and the arrests that followed at Kumbum. This parallels a phenomenon that a number of observers noted after China's violent suppression of its own democracy movement in June 1989. Those who dared to speak out truthfully and bluntly about the events in Beijing and elsewhere risked arrest and imprisonment for spreading counterrevolutionary rumors. So too, in areas of Eastern Tibet that have been the sites of demonstrations the same risk exists for Tibetans. Silence surrounds events there, and information is difficult to come by.

dramatically.[70] Since then, the arrests have continued, and trials of those accused of engaging in pro-independence activity over the past two years have taken place. Asia Watch is not aware that the rescinding of martial law has led to the release of any political prisoners in Tibet.

On November 30, 1989, ten monks from **Drepung** monastery were sentenced at a mass rally to terms ranging from five to nineteen years imprisonment for having organized a Tibetan independence group in January of the same year. Their activities included gathering information and mimeographing leaflets "for their foreign boss," according to Chinese reports. The monks were named as **Ngawang Buchung** (Ngag-dbang bu-chung), **Ngawang Osel** (Ngag-dbang 'od-gsal), **Kelsang Dhondup** (Skal-bzang don-grub), **Ngawang Gyaltsen** (Ngag-dbang rgyal-mtshan), **Jampel Chunjor** ('Jam-dpal chos-'byor), **Jampel Losel** ('Jam-dpal blo-gsal), **Ngawang Rinchen** (Ngag-dbang rin-chen), **Jampel Monlam** ('Jam-dpal smon-lam), **Jampel Tsering** ('Jam-dpal tshe-ring), and **Ngawang Gongar** (Ngag-dbang gong-dkar).

At the same time that the members of this group were sentenced, another Tibetan, **Dhondup Dorje** (Don-grub rdo-rje), was also sentenced to five years imprisonment for similarly "disseminating counterrevolutionary propaganda." He was not, however, a member of the same group as the Drepung monks.[71] The case of those monks fits in, unfortunately, with

---

[70] The case details of many of those arrested in Tibet since March 1989, including most of those whose arrests are discussed below, can be found in Asia Watch's recent report on China: *Punishment Season: Human Rights in China After Martial Law*, pp. 57-59.

[71] "Lhasa Court Sentences Counterrevolutionaries," *Xinhua*, December 1, 1989,; in *FBIS*, same day; and "'Counterrevolutionary' Lamas Sentenced in Lhasa," *Radio Lhasa*,

other instances that we have noted, in which the PRC authorities attempt to ascribe dissident activity to foreign manipulation. Pamphleteering has also been considered sufficient cause, in and of itself, for arrest and imprisonment; Tibetan exile sources have cited a September 29, 1988, Radio Lhasa broadcast describing the case of a 32-year-old bank employee, **Lhakpa Tsering** (Lhag-pa tshe-ring), who was arrested on September 28, 1988 as a counterrevolutionary for having written separatist leaflets and letters.

Tseten Norgye (Tshe-brtan nor-rgyas), approximately 45, was arrested in April or May after a police raid on his home uncovered a mimeograph machine on which Tibetan independence literature was said to have been printed. Amnesty International issued an Urgent Action notice about him, when it was reported that he was scheduled for execution. Asia Watch sent a cable to Chinese premier **Li Peng**, expressing concern about reports that Tseten Norgye had been tortured and was being denied contact with family members. We asked that he be released immediately unless he could be charged with a recognizable criminal offense, and urged that if he were not released that he be allowed visitors and that concerned observers be allowed access to the judicial proceedings in his case, which should be open and public.

Three Tibetans who had taken part in the March 1989 protests were sentenced to prison terms in October. They are **Tendar** (Bstan-dar), 18, from Medro Gongkar (Mal-gro gong-dkar), who received a six-year sentence; and **Dawa Tsering** (Zla-ba tshe-ring) 17, and **Dorje** (Rdo-rje), 24, both from Lhasa, who each received four-year sentences.

Tashi Tsering (Bkra-shis tshe-ring) a member of the **Shigatse** (Gzhis-ka-rtse) branch of the Chinese People's Political Consultative Congress has been charged with producing counterrevolutionary propaganda on account of his writing and

---

November 30, 1989, in *FBIS*, December 1, 1989.

distribution of slogans and leaflets in favor of Tibetan independence and against the socialist system and the Communist Party. He is reportedly now awaiting trial.

In November 1989, five monks, **Tenzin** (Bstan-'dzin), **Purgyal** (Phur-rgyal), **Lhagpa** (Lhag-pa), **Trinley** ('Phrin-las) and **"Lichuo"**[72] were sent to labor camps without trial for three years on account of their participation in demonstrations for Tibetan independence two months earlier. Apart from Tenzin, who is from **Ganden** monastery, the monks are all from the small monastery of **Dala Lupuk** (Brag-lha klu-phug), which lies close to the Potala. A sixth monk, also from Dala Lupuk, named **Dawa Tsering** (Zla-ba tshe-ring), is awaiting trial on charges of organizing separatist activities.

Five middle school students in Lhasa were arrested in December and charged with forming a counterrevolutionary organization that called for Tibetan independence, the "Young Lion Group." The five were named as **"Mina" Tsering** ([Mi-nyag?] Tshe-ring), **"Dalaba" Tsering** ([Zla-ba?] Tshe-ring), **"Zhonglaba" Tsering** ([?] Tshe-ring), **"Xiaobian" Tsering** ([?] Tshe-ring), and **Tashi Wangdu** (Bkra-shis dbang-'dus). Another student, **Phurbu** (Phur-bu), has been sentenced to undergo "reform through labor" for his participation in the group's activities.

Dawa Drolma (Zla-ba sgrol-ma), a temporary teacher at the Lhasa City Cement Plant, was given a suspended sentence after being charged with teaching her students a reactionary song and sheltering rioters. The sentence was suspended in consideration of the fact that she had a one-year-old son to care for.

Loye (Blo-ye), a monk at the **Potala**, was sentenced in December to 15 years imprisonment and 5 years deprivation of political rights for allegedly making counterrevolutionary

---

[72] Perhaps Rindrol (Rin-sgrol) or Rigdrol (Rig-sgrol); the actual Tibetan form is difficult to determine on the basis of the transcription given.

propaganda and espionage. He was accused of having collected intelligence "for the enemy abroad."

Four nuns, **Phuntsog Dzomgyal** (Phun-tshogs 'dzoms-rgyal), **Kesang Wangmo** (Skal-bzang dbang-mo), **Tenzin Chogyal** (Bstan-'dzin chos-rgyal), and **Tenzin Wangmo** (Bstan-'dzin dbang-mo), were arrested for having staged a small Tibetan independence demonstration on October 14 and sentenced to three years in labor re-education camps. Two other nuns from the **Michung** (Me-chung) nunnery, **Puntsog Nyidon** (Phun-tshogs nyi-sgron) and **Puntsog Pema** (Phun-tshogs padma), were accused of being the ringleaders of the group and are awaiting sentencing. Two more Tibetans who were accused of having shouted reactionary slogans on the same day, **Kesang Dolkar** (Skal-bzang sgrol-dkar) and **Tsegyal** (Tshe-rgyal), received two-year sentences. Two nuns who demonstrated one day later, **Lobsang Dolma** (Blo-bzang sgrol-ma) and **Ngawang Chodon** (Ngag-dbang chos-sgron) received three-year sentences of re-education through labor.

The arrests of two Tibetans, **Tenzin Puntsog** (Bstan-'dzin phun-tshogs), 33, and **Ngodrup Gyaltsen** (Dngos-grub rgyal-mtshan), 37, were reported in August. Both were said to have confessed to serving as agents of the Dalai Lama. Tenzin Puntsog is reportedly accused of urging on crowds to attack the police station in the **Barkor** area and of having distributed reactionary propaganda. Ngodrup Gyaltsen is said to be accused of doing intelligence work for the Dalai Lama. In September, however, it was reported that a monk from the monastery of **Drepung, Ngawang Gyaltsen** (Ngag-dbang rgyal-mtshan), had been sentenced to a five-year prison term for having passed on information to Tenzin Puntsog, described as an intelligence agent for the Dalai Lama.

Seven other Tibetans were tried and sentenced for their involvement in the March disturbances. **Tsering Ngodrup** (Tshe-ring dngos-grub), 57, was sentenced to 12 years imprisonment, accused of being a spy for the Dalai Lama and making counterrevolutionary propaganda. **"Dagwa"**[73], a lama at **Rato** monastery, was sentenced to four years for similarly inciting people, hanging the banned Tibetan flag and shouting reactionary slogans. **Namkha** (Nam-mkha'), also a lama at Rato, received a three-year sentence for the same offenses. Three other Tibetans, **"Dingling,"**[74] **Dagwa,**[75] and **Kesang** (Skal-bzang), received prison sentences of five, eight, and four years, respectively, for charges stemming from participation in the March unrest. Another Tibetan named **Pasang** (Pa-sangs) received a life sentence for essentially the same offenses.

Imprisonment and the scale of political detention

An account of life in a Tibetan prison, written by two visiting Chinese reporters, appeared in an official Chinese magazine in late 1988.[76] Consistent with the official line taken since the resurgence in 1987 of widespread international interest in human rights conditions in Tibet, the article states that there are only one prison and two labor reform camps in the entire region.[77] It relates the story of a prisoner named **Tenzin**

---

[73] Either Dawa (Zla-ba) or Dagpa (Dag-pa); the actual Tibetan form is difficult to determine on the basis of the transcription given.

[74] The actual Tibetan form of this name is difficult to determine on the basis of the transcription given.

[75] Not the person of the same name mentioned earlier in this paragraph.

[76] Liu Zhiquan and Yang Xinhe, "Xizang jianyu jianwen," *Liaowang* (Overseas Edition), November 28, 1988.

[77] See *Human Rights in Tibet* (Asia Watch), p. 32.

Chodak (Bstan-'dzin chos-grags), who was sentenced as a counter-revolutionary in 1983 to 12 years in prison for separatist activities. According to the report, he is allowed family visits once a month, and he can write letters to family and friends, albeit subject to inspection and supervision by the authorities. The prison is said to subscribe to a number of periodicals in Tibetan and Chinese that the inmates can read. The article specifically mentions that Tenzin Chodak has not been tortured; and moreover, that channels exist for filing grievances in cases of mistreatment.

Thus far in his term of imprisonment, Tenzin Chodak is said to have been allowed to undertake a Tibet University self-study course and related examinations. The article describes a diversity of cultural and recreational activities in the prison, including movies, competitive games, and dances; the prison work performed by the inmates is said to include gardening and also the repair of cars and machinery. Tibetan prisoners reportedly receive butter, tea and fixed sums of money for purchases from the prison store. In addition, the article states that there is free medical treatment available in the prison, while for serious illnesses outside hospital care is made available. The late **Geshe Lobsang Wangchuk**, a well-known activist who died while serving a long sentence,[78] supposedly availed himself of this enlightened policy prior to his death, according to the article.

The prison that is the subject of this report is not specifically named, but it is said to be in the northern suburbs of Lhasa. That fact, and the reference to Geshe Lobsang Wangchuk as one of its previous inmates, leads us to assume that the prison in question is **Drapchi** (Grwa-bzhi), one of several in the Lhasa area, and one known to hold a number of political prisoners.

This official account of life in Drapchi is strongly at variance with the accounts of political imprisonment in Tibet gathered by Asia Watch from other sources. For example, the

---

[78] His case was prominently featured in *Human Rights in Tibet*, pp. 33-36.

article quoted a Tibetan described as being the head of the labor reform office of the TAR, one **Kelsang** (Skal-bzang, or Gesang in Chinese), as saying that there were only 1044 prisoners in Tibet, of whom only 18 were counterrevolutionaries. Of these, eight were actually only common hooligans and thieves, but had been classed as counterrevolutionaries because they had provoked disturbances in prison.

Thus, by this account, only 10 Tibetans could truly be called political prisoners. While this figure refers to the situation in Tibet prior to the imposition of martial law in Lhasa, all of the independent information available to Asia Watch indicates that it was a gross underestimate then, and it certainly bears little relationship to the true scale of political imprisonment in Tibet now. A Western journalist who visited Tibet in late 1989 quoted an unnamed Tibetan who worked in the Public Security Bureau as saying that more than 1000 Tibetans were imprisoned in Lhasa, with the implication that these were political prisoners.[79]

As we noted in our previous reports on the subject, the notion of there being only one prison and two labor camps in Tibet is not credible. The fact is that the Chinese government simply does not list many of its detention facilities in the region as being official prisons. For example, Tibetan exile sources refer to one of the prisons in the Lhasa area by the name **"Utitod"**, which is most likely a Tibetan rendering of the Chinese term *Wuzhidui*: "No. 5 Detachment." This facility is said by them to be functionally a part of **Sangyip** (Gsang-yib) Prison. According to other Tibetans, though, the name "Sangyip Prison" is itself an unofficial Tibetan designation for the facility; the Chinese themselves do not officially recognize it as being a prison. Hence the two names and the resultant confusion.

This disingenuous reliance on official categories is the basis for Chinese insistence that there are only one prison and two

---

[79] Guy Dinmore, "China Denies Allegations of Prison Beatings, Torture in Tibet," *Reuters*, October 22, 1989.

labor camps in the TAR. It is akin to persistent Chinese claims that there are only 73,000 Chinese in the TAR, when any visitor can see that there are far more than that in the Lhasa area alone. This sort of legerdemain with figures cannot conceal the fact that detention and imprisonment in Tibet is not limited to one prison and two labor camps. Asia Watch believes that the Chinese authorities purposely seek to obscure information about the prison situation in Tibet in order to evade criticism for conditions that are in violation of accepted human rights standards.

4. Trials of Political Prisoners

In *Evading Scrutiny*, we noted Asia Watch's request to the Chinese government to be allowed to send qualified observers to the trials of four students accused in the death of a police official. The Chinese government refused.[80] The four accused in the case, **Lobsang Tenzin** (Blo-bzang bstan-'dzin), **Tsering Dhondup** (Tshe-ring don-grub), **Sonam Wangdu** (Bsod-nams dbang-'dus), and **Gyaltsen Chophel** (Rgyal-mtshan chos-'phel), were placed on trial with two others, **Tamdin** (Rta-mgrin) and **Pakto** (Bag-gro), who presumably were also arrested for participation in the March 1988 protest. Chinese press statements noted that their guilt had already been determined, but trials were nonetheless held and an account of one day's proceedings was published in the Tibetan exile press.[81]

The day's proceedings against the six prisoners began at 10:30 on the morning of January 9, 1989, in the assembly hall of the Armed Police Regiment (Drag-chas nyen-rtogs ru-chen, or Wuzhuang Jingcha Dadui in Chinese) in Lhasa. An atmosphere of considerable tension seems to have marked the trial. The path from the main gate of the compound to the door of the assembly hall was reportedly lined with armed police, armed security personnel and court workers. The requirement that spectators must hold passes was strictly enforced. On the platform in the hall

---

[80] *Evading Scrutiny* (Asia Watch), p. 7.

[81] "Khrims-rwa'i thog-gi 'thab-rtsod," *Shes-bya*, February, 1989, pp. 11-12 and 27. Trials in Tibet have traditionally been highly secretive, but the authorities recently began announcing "public" trials - although no foreign observers are permitted to attend. Friends and relatives, however, have been able to witness the proceedings and to know something of the conditions of the accused.

was a judge from the Lhasa Intermediate People's Court, to his right and left were two investigators and a secretary; and to their right was a case investigator from the Lhasa People's Procuratorate and a female secretary. To their left were Lobsang Tenzin's two elder brothers, staff workers at Tibet's daily newspaper who were there to argue in their brother's defense. Also in attendance were relatives of the defendants who had managed to get passes, together with approximately 200 unarmed security personnel and 100 reporters, photographers and other representatives of the Chinese media.

The presiding judge opened the proceedings and called for the defendants to be brought in. With Chinese armed police force personnel on either side holding their arms, the six defendants were roughly led in with their heads pushed down. A number of photographs were taken of them. The judge read the charges, stemming from their participation in the March violence, and then asked them if they admitted their guilt. The six said that not only did they not admit their guilt to the many charges against them, but that admissions of guilt supplied by them in prison had in fact been coercively extracted from them while they were first manacled, and then beaten and tortured beyond physical endurance. They furthermore called upon the authorities to investigate the charges that they, the prisoners, were now making. The account says little more about the proceedings beyond this point, except to imply that they were somewhat disrupted by the statements of the defendants and to further note that the six of them were, as a result, severely beaten on their way back to prison after the session.

We should emphasize again that this account comes from a Tibetan exile publication and we are unable independently to verify it. We believe that it is credible, however, as it accords substantially with other reliable information about political imprisonment in Tibet, as outlined in Asia Watch's previous two reports on the region. Tibetans have told us that they are afforded no independent legal counsel when brought to trial, nor can they mount anything that might reasonably be recognized as being a proper legal defense. The use of torture, mentioned in the account, is unfortunately (as will be discussed below) an all-too-familiar feature in cases of political imprisonment and interrogation in Tibet.

It was announced on January 19, 1989, ten days after the hearing, that **Lobsang Tenzin** had been given a death sentence with a two-year suspension of execution. Another one of the four accused, **Sonam Wangdu**, was sentenced to life imprisonment. Various other Tibetans were also sentenced at the same time and received sentences ranging from three to fifteen years imprisonment.[82]

In addition, the group sentenced on January 19 included **Yulo Dawa Tsering** (Gyu-lo Zla-ba tshe-ring), a lama from the monastery of Ganden (Dga'-ldan) who is currently perhaps the most well-known Tibetan political prisoner. Arrested in December 1987 for having "spread reactionary views, such as Tibetan independence, to foreign reactionary elements who came to Tibet as tourists,"[83] he was subsequently accused of having "colluded with reactionaries abroad to try to overthrow the people's government and the socialist system,"[84] and was eventually charged with the crime of spreading counterrevolutionary propaganda.[85]

---

[82] "Lhasa Rioters Are Sentenced," *Beijing Review*, January 30 - February 5, 1989; and "Tibetans Sentenced for Role in March 1988 Riots," *Xinhua*, January 19, 1989, in *FBIS*, January 23.

[83] *Evading Scrutiny*, p. 10.

[84] "Tibetan Buddhists Charged With Counterrevolution," *Xinhua*, September 21, 1989; in *FBIS*, same day.

[85] *Evading Scrutiny*, p. 6.

According to Tibetan exile sources and others,[86] the real reason for his continued detention concerns comments that he made to a visiting Italian, **Dr. Stefano Dallari,** who videotaped a conversation with him and another monk, **Thubten Tsering** (Thub-bstan tshe-ring), during which he made strong remarks in favor of Tibetan independence. He received a sentence of 14 years imprisonment.[87]

The group sentenced probably also included **Chungdag** (Chung-bdag), a monk from the monastery of Ganden (Dga'-ldan), who received a seven-year prison sentence for participation in the 1987 protests and was expelled from the Tibet branch of the China Buddhist Association along with Yulo Dawa Tsering in September 1989.[88]

In February 1990, Tibetan exile sources reported that Lobsang Tenzin was slated for imminent execution. According to these reports, the two-year reprieve granted him was meant to be effective from the date of his arrest (although Chinese sources have not confirmed this). Amnesty International issued an Urgent Action/Fear of Execution alert concerning Lobsang Tenzin, while Asia Watch cabled Chinese Prime Minister Li Peng on February 22, 1990 stating that, given the circumstances of his trial, he had clearly not received a fair and impartial hearing, and that therefore he should not be subjected to execution.

On March 16, 1990, the Chinese Embassy in Washington issued a statement that "Lobsang Tengin [sic] was...the principal culprit in the murder of a member of the armed police....He was found guilty and sentenced to death with a two-year repriev [sic]

---

[86] An Urgent Action notice sent out by Amnesty International and an appeal from the Tibetan exile authorities. Amnesty UA ASA 17/03/89.

[87] "27 Rioters Sentenced," *Tibetan Review*, February 1989, p.5.

[88] "Tibetan Buddhists Charged With Counterrevolution," *Xinhua*, September 21, 1989; in *FBIS*, same day.

by the People's Court of the Municipality of Lhasa on January 23, 1989. The rumour that 'he will be executed in March 1990' is purely fabricated." We would note that a death sentence still hangs over Lobsang Tenzin.

5. Use of Torture against Prisoners

Asia Watch is seriously concerned about conditions of detention for political prisoners in Tibet, particularly in regard to the use of torture. By all accounts, torture is widely practiced by the region's security forces. Both of our previous reports on Tibet documented cases of torture, and many similar accounts have since been presented both by the foreign media and by Tibetan exile sources. The PRC in 1988 ratified the United Nations' *Convention Against Torture and Other Cruel, Inhuman or Degrading Treatment or Punishment*, thereby assuming an international obligation to refrain from:

> ...any act by which severe pain or suffering, whether physical or mental, is intentionally inflicted on a person...by or at the instigation of or with the consent of or acquiescence of a public official or other person acting in an official capacity. (Article 1)

Under the terms of this convention, the PRC authorities are required to investigate allegations of torture fully and fairly, and to duly punish those responsible. In addition, the government should be called upon to ensure that access to Tibet for concerned observers should be unhindered, and to facilitate independent monitoring of the situation. China's ratification of the UN's Convention Against Torture imposes solemn legal obligations upon China which the international community has a legitimate interest in seeing kept. China's claim that the persistent allegations of torture in Tibetan prisons represent foreign interference in China's internal affairs is thus untenable.

Accounts of torture in Tibetan prisons are fairly numerous. Although a certain proportion of these come from Tibetan exile sources, they differ very little from those obtained from independent journalists and from other reports that Asia Watch has previously been able to verify. During the visit of Senator Leahy's group to Tibet in August 1988, for example, Tibetans told the group members and journalists accompanying them of various forms of torture that had been used against participants in the demonstrations in 1987 and 1988.[89] One of the accompanying journalists reported an account given to him by a recently released monk concerning the conditions of imprisonment that Tibetan political prisoners had endured in the aftermath of the March 1988 protest in Lhasa. The monk told of savage beatings by the police, administered with fists, feet, sticks and rifle butts, resulting in broken bones, hearing loss and other such traumas. In addition, he described the application of shocks with electric cattle prods, and the suspension of prisoners by ropes, often resulting in dislocation of the shoulders. The monk also revealed that those treated most harshly were nuns who had taken part in the demonstrations.[90] Similar stories have been told to other visitors as well.[91]

The full transcript of the monk's account, obtained from Tibetan exile sources, contains the following details. The monk was held in **Gutsa** (Dgu-rtsa) prison, one of the prisons in the Lhasa region mentioned in our first report on human rights conditions in Tibet.[92] He was held in a room approximately six feet by 10 feet with six other prisoners. Their food consisted of the

---

[89] Daniel Southerland, "3 Senators Query Chinese On Tibetan Human Rights," *The Washington Post*, August 26, 1988.

[90] Daniel Southerland, "Tibetan Tells of Torture," *The Washington Post*, September 6, 1988.

[91] See J. Michael Luhan, "How the Chinese Rule Tibet," *Dissent*, Winter 1989; Mark Baker, "The Ugly Side of Tibet," *The Herald* (Australia), July 26, 1988; and "Prisoners in Tibet Beaten and Tortured," *The South China Morning Post*, November 2, 1988.

[92] See *Human Rights in Tibet*, p. 32.

black tea, plain bread rolls and meager boiled vegetables that we saw mentioned in another Tibetan's account of his imprisonment in our first report.[93] Prisoners who had been tried and sentenced were allowed visitors, but other prisoners were denied this right; indeed, their relatives were never informed by the authorities as to their whereabouts.

According to the monk, he and all his cellmates were severely beaten at the time of their arrest. In addition, prisoners were verbally abused and ordered to admit their guilt and to name other participants in the demonstration. According to the monk, prisoners were told (regarding their advocacy of Tibetan independence): "You are all doing these things under the influence of a few bad foreigners..." The majority of the officials carrying out the beatings were Tibetans, according to the monk; in his case a Tibetan and a Chinese beat him while another Tibetan named **Phurbu** (Phur-bu), around 30 years old and from the **Chushul** (Chu-shul) area south of Lhasa, questioned him.

Tibetan exile sources have provided extensive information on torture, most of which is consistent with information obtained elsewhere by Asia Watch. A Tibetan exile who accompanied several Italian journalists in Lhasa as they sought out former detainees recounted the case of a nun who had been arrested after taking part in demonstrations in April 1988. Placed in **Gutsa** prison, she was beaten and attacked by dogs under the control of her guards. Her diet was restricted to the meager rations of bread rolls and boiled vegetables that we mentioned earlier. Another nun whom she encountered in prison told her of being subjected to torture with an electric cattle prod that included the application of the instrument to her genitals. Others with whom the Tibetan exile spoke were also subjected to severe beatings and torture with an electric cattle prod.

Various letters and documents from Tibet describing the situation of prisoners have been circulated by Tibetan exile

---

[93] See *Human Rights in Tibet*, p. 29.

authorities. One concerns a group of nuns from the **Gari** (Dga'-ri) and **Shongseb** (Gshong-gseb) nunneries in the Lhasa area imprisoned in **Gutsa**. Nuns from these convents, along with nuns from the **Chusang** (Chu-bzang) nunnery, also in the Lhasa vicinity, demonstrated in the Tibetan capital several times in April 1988. According to the letter, one nun named **Gyaltsen Chondzom** (Rgyal-mtshan chos-'dzoms) was severely beaten while manacled and had dogs set upon her in prison. Another nun from **Shongseb** was forced to kneel on ice for a long period and was tortured with an electric cattle prod that was applied to various parts of her body, including the genital area.

Similarly, in a Channel 4 (UK) television broadcast on November 9, 1988, a group of nuns interviewed in Tibet after their release from prison described having been stripped and then poked with electric cattle prods.[94] Another account of the arrest of these nuns that appeared in the West in 1989 detailed beatings, the application of electric cattle prods, attacks by trained dogs, and other forms of torture perpetrated on one nun during interrogation, as questioners sought to make her name others involved in planning the demonstration.[95]

---

[94] Nancy Banks-Smith, "Facing a Land of Fear," *The Guardian*, November 11, 1988; the article discusses the documentary film by Vanya Kewley: "Tibet — A Case to Answer," which appeared in Channel 4's "Dispatches" series.

[95] "'Some used electric sticks, some beat us over the head with handcuffs, some beat us with rifles'," *The Guardian*, November 8, 1989. Most recently Tibetan exile sources have claimed that three of the four nuns interviewed for the Channel 4 broadcast have been arrested again. They are named as Tenzin Wangmo (Bstan-'dzin dbang-mo), Gyaltsen Yangzom (Rgyal-mtshan dbyangs-'dzoms), and Gyaltsen Lochoe (Rgyal-mtshan blo-gros). Another nun, Gyaltsen Chokyi (Rgyal-mtshan chos-skyid), was also arrested with them. The whereabouts of the fourth man, Tsering Dolma

Another letter in this batch of material dealt with the case of **Gyaltsen Chopel**, one of the four Tibetans arrested for the murder of a police official during the March 1988 protest. (Gyaltsen Chopel's trial proceedings were summarized in the previous chapter.) The letter noted that he and almost all others arrested in the wake of the March 1988 protest were subjected to harsh beatings. At the time the letter was written (August 1988) his wounds were said to be healing, which may indicate that the torture, aimed at extracting a confession of guilt, had been applied in the earliest stages of imprisonment.

In the fall of 1989, the US organization Physicians for Human Rights published a report on torture and imprisonment in Tibet, based on interviews with Tibetans in India undertaken with the assistance of the Tibetan exile authorities. Those interviewed had been arrested during the demonstrations in Tibet in 1987 and 1988. The report detailed prison conditions and patterns of torture, including the use of beatings, electric cattle prods, prolonged suspension by ropes and other methods.[96]

Yet another account was transmitted through Tibetan exile sources, from a prisoner who was among those released in the summer of 1988. He also describes the use of electric cattle prods, suspension by ropes for hours at a time, beatings, and also the infliction of cigarette burns and scalding with boiling water. While it is impossible to verify all of these practices without better access to Tibet and Tibetan prisons, a consistent pattern of the use of torture against political prisoners is, we believe, now well established.

Some months after the imposition of martial law in Lhasa in March 1989, a British journalist, interviewing Tibetans who had

----

(Tshe-ring sgrol-ma), are not known. See "Nuns Interviewed in Kewley Film Arrested," *Tibetan Review*, April, 1990, p.4.

[96] John Ackerly and Blake Kerr, *The Suppression of a People: Accounts of Torture and Imprisonment in Tibet*, Physicians for Human Rights, November 1989.

been released from prison, was told of a female university student who had been crippled as a result of beatings sustained during her imprisonment. She had been arrested after the imposition of martial law for having put up Tibetan independence posters. He was also able to interview Tibetans who bore scars that they said were left by prison torture. One of them told of having his arm tied behind his back by the thumb for three days after his arrest, and of then being tortured with an electric cattle prod as interrogators tried to force him to name people involved in leading the March 1989 protests.[97] Another reporter encountered a monk who had been held for four months in solitary confinement after the March violence and tortured with electric cattle prods and beatings.[98]

In November 1989 Tibetan exile authorities reported the death in prison of **Chonze Tenpa Chophel** (Chos-mdzad Bstan-pa chos-'phel) on August 25, due to torture. Chonze had been arrested on November 15, 1987, for possession of a copy of the Dalai Lama's autobiography. His wife had previously been imprisoned, as had a son **Lobsang Chodak** (Blo-bsang chos-grags), who was adopted as a prisoner of conscience by Amnesty International during the period of his imprisonment several years ago. Lobsang Chodak was shot in the legs during the December 1988 Human Rights Day demonstration and is said to have been crippled. A daughter, **Nyima Tsamchoe** (Nyi-ma mtshams-gcod, also known as **Lhakdon** [Lhag-sgron]), has been imprisoned for over a year.[99] It is likely that the family's

---

[97] Guy Dinmore, "China Denies Allegations of Prison Beatings, Torture in Tibet," *Reuters*, October 22, 1989.

[98] Lewis M. Simons, "A Populace Seethes," *The Boston Globe*, December 7, 1989.

[99] "Bod-nang rgyal-gces dpa'-bo bsad dang gsod-rgyu'i skyo-gnas," *Shes-bya*, November, 1989, p. 15. Nyima Tsamchoe was

longstanding record of dissidence accounts for the particularly harsh treatment reportedly meted out to Chonze.

Asia Watch concludes that the political imprisonment of Tibetans who advocate independence for Tibet remains a particularly serious area of human rights violations, and one which the Chinese government shows no intention of handling in a manner compatible with international standards of respect for human rights. The grave nature of such abuses in Tibet is compounded by persistent, credible reports of the use of torture against political prisoners in the region. China's response to legitimate international concern in this matter has been aimed at obfuscating the problem. Having criminalized peaceful dissent about Tibet's political status and about Chinese policies in the area, the Chinese authorities simply deny that political imprisonment and torture take place there at all.

A Western journalist who visited Lhasa in October 1989, for example, was told by **Wang Naiwen**, spokesman for the TAR regional Public Security Bureau: "We have strict rules and regulations. All prisoners receive fair treatment. No one has been beaten or tortured. I am absolutely sure of this."[100] Rather than adopting effective preventive and remedial measures, the Chinese authorities have instead taken strenuous steps to insure that concerned outside observers are denied, for the most part, any real possibility of investigating conditions in Tibetan prisons.

---

listed as number 58 on the list of prisoners appended to *Evading Scrutiny*.

[100] Guy Dinmore, "China Denies Allegations of Prison Beatings, Torture in Tibet," *Reuters*, October 22, 1989.

6. Restrictions on Contact between Foreigners and Tibetan Dissidents

Periodically, the Chinese authorities have claimed that foreigners were intimately involved in the planning and execution of demonstrations in Tibet. Since the recent round of demonstrations began, in September 1987, the Chinese authorities have shown mounting hostility toward individual travelers in Tibet, and have undertaken a series of measures apparently designed to prevent foreign observers from witnessing human rights abuses in the region.

First, in the wake of the demonstrations of late 1987, all tourists were rounded up and ordered out of Lhasa, leaving only a handful of Westerners, mostly teachers and researchers, in the area. A prohibition on individual tourists (that is, those not in chaperoned tourist groups) was then imposed, in an attempt to effectively deny Tibetan dissidents a conduit to the outside world and thereby institute a monopoly on information coming out of Tibet. For a period this move did have the practical effect of blocking individual tourists to any large degree from spending time in Tibet. Eventually, though, people began to get around this policy by a variety of means, including that of forming themselves into very small groups just prior to visiting Tibet. Sometimes composed of only one couple, these groups were able to stay in the cheaper hotels in the Tibetan quarter, as opposed to the more expensive hotels such as that run by Holiday Inn, which are located well away from the quarter. By the summer and fall of 1988, the presence of individual Western tourists in Lhasa had once more grown, although the level was nowhere as high as before. After the imposition of martial law in Lhasa, individual tourism to the region again virtually ceased.

In order to curtail free dialogue between Tibetan dissidents and the outside world, foreigners have been subjected to deliberate harassment. A British worker in Lhasa during the period after the first demonstrations in the fall of 1987 described the hostility toward foreigners exhibited by the authorities as being akin to a witch hunt, with local TAR television broadcast footage of foreigners standing in the vicinity of demonstrations, a pair of British teachers having their home ransacked prior to being placed under house arrest and expelled, and Lhasa students being subjected to a campaign of negative lectures and propaganda about foreigners.[101] It goes without saying that Tibetans who are believed to have done no more than inform foreigners about Tibetan dissatisfaction with China's presence in Tibet, or about human rights abuses in the region, have been harshly treated.

Perhaps the most striking example of official hostility towards foreigners in Tibet occurred in connection with the December 10, 1988 Human Rights Day protest in Lhasa, wherein a 26-year-old Dutch woman was wounded. Early Chinese reports on the incident seemed to insinuate that she was in some measure to blame for her wound simply for having been in the vicinity of the demonstration; furthermore, both the fact that she had visited Tibet repeatedly during 1988 and her possession of a copy of the Dalai Lama's autobiography were also held to be suspicious.[102] In March of last year her case was once more brought up by the Chinese authorities in the wake of the violence that preceded the imposition of martial law. **Yan Mingfu**, a senior Communist Party official, accused her of entering Tibet several times under various pseudonyms in order to organize the December 10 "riot" at the behest of an overseas separatist group.

---

[101] Julie Brittain, "Britain Bows to Chinese in Tibet Teacher Project," *The Hongkong Standard*, August 6, 1988.

[102] See Nicholas D. Kristof, "China Reports One Monk Killed in Tibet Clash," *The New York Times*, December 12, 1988; "Situation Tense; Dutch Woman Held," *AFP*, December 12, 1988; in *FBIS*, same day; and "Says Netherlander Can Leave Tibet," *Xinhua*, December 15, 1988; in *FBIS*, same day.

Moreover, Yan Mingfu's remark to the effect that "this information was offered by Tibetan patriots and this showed that most Tibetan lamas are patriotic"[103] gives grounds for serious concern as to the manner in which such information is obtained from Tibetans, and particularly from prisoners who were arrested immediately after the March 1989 violence. Chinese press reports, for example, described the voluntary surrender of people who had participated in the protests and who then proceeded to inform against other participants.[104] A more recent British press story, drawn from interviews with nuns who had been arrested following a demonstration in Lhasa in April 1988, described the beating of the nuns when they would not or could not answer, to the satisfaction of their interrogators, questions as to who had been behind their protest.[105]

Following the December 10 demonstration, the movements of foreigners in Lhasa were sharply restricted. A number of reports indicated that foreigners were confined to their hotel rooms and that the rooms were searched by security personnel. According to one report, the police were searching for foreign journalists in particular,[106] while another said that they were

---

[103] "Comment on Martial Law," *Xinhua*, March 21, 1989; in *FBIS*, March 22.

[104] See "Rioters Surrender to Police," *Xinhua*, March 9, 1989, published in *Renmin Ribao* on March 10, in *FBIS*, March 10; and "Streets Remain Quiet," *Renmin Ribao*, March 11, 1989, in *FBIS*, March 13.

[105] "'Some used electric sticks, some beat us over the head with handcuffs, some beat us with rifles'," *The Guardian*, November 8, 1989.

[106] Danny Gittings, "Tibetans Killed by China Police," *The Guardian*, December 12, 1988.

looking for any foreigners who had witnessed the demonstration.[107]

Actions directed at foreign journalists attempting to report on events and conditions in Tibet have also been noticeable. As we mentioned in our earlier reports, journalists have been expelled from Lhasa and barred from entering Tibet except in rare instances. In an incident in Beijing a few days after the Human Rights Day demonstration, a reporter was held for two hours by the authorities for attempting to cover a march by Tibetan students in the Chinese capital protesting the government's violent suppression of the Lhasa demonstration.[108] On December 30, 1988, a further demonstration was held in Lhasa by Tibetan students calling on the authorities to respect Tibetan culture and to stop using firearms against Tibetans. Three Western tourists who tried to photograph the demonstration were stopped by Chinese security personnel and eventually made to surrender their film and pay fines for violating regulations against photographing demonstrations. One of them reported having been held by plainclothes security forces at gunpoint.[109]

In an apparent reaction to a British television broadcast highly critical of China's record in Tibet, which had been filmed surreptitiously by someone travelling through various Tibetan areas in the TAR and in neighboring provinces, unauthorized

---

[107] "Tibetan Riot Results in 1 Death, 13 Injuries, Tighter Chinese Rule," *The Washington Times*, December 12, 1988.

[108] Nicholas D. Kristof, "Tibetans Hold Protest in Beijing," *The New York Times*, December 19, 1988.

[109] "Two Injured in 30 Dec Demonstration in Tibet," *The Hong Kong Standard*, in *FBIS*, January 3, 1989; Daniel Southerland, "Students Defy Protest Ban in Tibetan City," *The Washington Post*, January, 1, 1989; and Robbie Barnett, "Police Grab Tourist in Tibet Protest," *The Independent*, January 2, 1989.

filming in Tibet was banned by the authorities in late March 1989.[110] In a related act, just a few days later, a correspondent for Agence France-Presse had his Chinese press credentials suspended for one month for having gone to Tibet without authorization. Two British reporters were similarly given warnings as a result of their unauthorized trips to the region.[111]

The authorities' conspiracy theory as to the true nature of foreign concern about human rights abuses in Tibet was spelled out in an article explaining the reasons for the imposition of martial law:

> Facts over the years have proved that with the opening of the Tibet Autonomous region to the outside world, some former Tibetan separatists now residing abroad and a handful of foreigners who do not understand China's minority nationality problem and the history of Tibet, have come to Tibet to carry out activities under the banner of "protecting human rights." Their purpose is to sow discord among the Tibetan compatriots and undermine unity between the Han and Tibetan nationalities.

---

[110] "Tibet Bans Unapproved Shooting of TV Films," *Radio Lhasa*, March 20, 1989; in *FBIS*, March 21. In addition, videotapes of disturbances in Tibet made by foreigners who just happened to be in Lhasa when they occurred have occasionally appeared on Western television. More recently a videotape made by Tibetan security personnel of the demonstration and ensuing violence that broke out in Lhasa on March 5, 1988, was gotten out of Tibet. Parts of it, showing Chinese personnel severely beating unarmed monks was shown on the American program "20/20" in the spring of 1989.

[111] "Reporter Accused of Violating Martial Law," *AFP*, March 22, 1989; in *FBIS*, March 23.

The same old method is used almost every time by the separatists in stirring up trouble. They make use of religious relations to incite some lamas and nuns to go into the streets and demonstrate, flaunt the banner of the "Snow Mountain and Lion," shout slogans of "independence for Tibet," instigate the masses to provoke Han compatriots, and then beat, smash, loot, and burn the houses and property of the Hans and the Tibetan compatriots who refuse to join them and destroy the offices of government departments and mass organizations.

They attack the public security personnel who come to persuade them to observe public order and force the public security personnel to counterattack in self-defense. Then they instigate the masses to join the riot and "condemn" the "savage act" of the Hans in the presence of foreigners in order that the foreigners will take photographs of the incident and carry them in the press abroad, which will become a "momentum" to their advantage.[112]

The extreme danger courted by Tibetan dissidents who meet with foreign visitors is illustrated by the case of **Yulo Dawa Tsering**, the lama from the monastery of **Ganden** reportedly arrested for speaking with foreigners about independence. His imprisonment, together with another monk, Tubten Tsering (Thub-bstan tshe-ring), solely for their peaceful expression of views at variance with official Chinese policy in the region, illustrates the rigor and determination with which the authorities approach the task of cutting Tibetan dissidents off from avenues for communicating their sentiments to the outside world.

---

[112] "Necessity of Martial Law Viewed," *Ta Kung Pao*, March 8, 1989; in *FBIS*, same day.

In December 1989, the secretary of the Tibet International Travel Service stated that restrictions prohibiting individual travel in Tibet will remain in effect for another two or three years.[113] Subsequently, supervised groups were allowed in, but only in conformity with martial law regulations; that is, they were only allowed to enter the Tibetan quarter of the city with appropriate passes and in the company of official Chinese personnel. For all practical purposes, therefore, access to Tibet is far more restricted now than it was in the period prior to the fall of 1987, for both tourists and journalists. The lifting of martial law has not altered the government's determination to maintain restrictions on travel in Tibet. On May 7 of this year the Tibetan regional government announced travel restrictions that now require all foreigners travelling to Tibet to make arrangements with and obtain permission from official organs for any travel to Tibet, above and beyond any other visa formalities for travel in the PRC.[114]

---

[113] "Restrictions on Foreign Travel in Tibet Eased," *Xinhua*, December 8, 1989; in *FBIS*, December 11.

[114] "Xizang xuanbu waiguoren jin Zang giuding," *Renmin ribao*, May 8, 1990.

II. CULTURAL REPRESSION

7. Suppression of Religious Freedom

Freedom of religion in Tibet is restricted in numerous ways by the authorities. Control of Buddhism as both an intellectual and a political force has taken on greater significance since the beginning of the recent series of demonstrations in the fall of 1987. Monks have played a significant leading role in many (but not all) of these demonstrations, contributing an ever-growing air of nationalism to the practice of Tibetan Buddhism in an officially atheist Chinese state. The desire of the PRC authorities to exert tighter controls over Buddhism in Tibet is thus perhaps unsurprising. Asia Watch believes that these controls, which ultimately derive from the Chinese authorities' adamant refusal to allow any free expression and dissent on Tibet's major political issues, seriously interfere with the free practice of Buddhism in Tibet as Buddhists there wish to practice it.

The Chinese authorities have often made clear their view that some controls over the Buddhist clergy are necessary in order to develop among them a more reliable sense of allegiance to the Chinese state. As we noted in *Human Rights in Tibet*, monastic finances are generally under the control of governmental authorities, and persistent efforts have been made to keep Buddhism as an intellectual force in check through the imposition of controls on the availability of teachings and their propagation, and through state-imposed limits on monastic ordination. More recent measures have included the introduction of a more conspicuous government role in the actual training of monks, via the establishment of government-led religious training institutions and the establishment of various state-controlled supervisory bodies.

On June 6, 1988, the Chinese Tibetan-Language Academy for Higher Buddhist Studies (*Zhongguo Zangyuxi Gaoji Foxueyuan*)

65

produced its first graduates, a group of 37 incarnate lamas who had completed a nine-and-a-half-month course that included studies of religion, science and politics. In a clear warning against the temptations of monastic involvement in the banned Tibetan independence movement, the **Panchen Lama**, officiating at the graduation, exhorted the assembled graduates to "become patriotic and law-abiding" lamas.[115] Similarly, a Tibetan radio broadcast in December that year, discussing the work of the regional Nationalities Religious Affairs Commission, stated that the commission members had "set greater store on education in patriotism and in the legal system among Buddhist monks and nuns and publicized the idea of placing patriotism first and love for religion second."[116] Until recently the authorities appeared to have been allowing gradual increases in the monastic population in various Tibetan areas of the PRC, but the situation since the introduction of martial law in the Lhasa area remains unclear. Certainly, entry into the monastic community is not a decision taken solely by the aspiring monk or nun and the Buddhist establishment concerned, for governmental authority intrudes into the decision.

On September 28, 1988, the late Panchen Lama announced the forthcoming establishment of a "Tibetan Buddhism Guidance Committee" (*Zangchuan Fojiao Zhidao Weiyuanhui*), to be under his leadership, and designed (among other things) "to bring up intellectuals specializing in Buddhism.....[and] educate monks and nuns to be patriotic and to observe the law....." He also stressed:

> [I]t is necessary to educate [monks and nuns] to love the country and abide by its laws. This is the least one expects of a citizen. The political

---

[115] "Banchan yaoqiu huofo aiguo shoufa," *Renmin Ribao*, June 15, 1988.

[116] "Tibet Civil Servants Condemn Splittism," *Radio Lhasa*, December 13, 1988; in *FBIS*, December 14.

tendencies of monks and nuns in Tibet as well as other regions are very important to the stability and unity of the locality. It was precisely with monks and nuns taking the lead that disturbances erupted in Lhasa this year as well as last year.[117]

Although this approach is sometimes contrasted against the hardline approach taken by Chinese leaders such as Qiao Shi, one should note that even here the Panchen Lama emphasized the basic illegality of any activities in support of Tibetan independence, regardless of their nature, as well as (by extension) the right of the state to arrest those involved. According to the article:

[The Panchen Lama] stressed that no leniency will be shown to those who have persisted in splittism, starting and stirring up troubles, and we will force them to accept education. It is important to weed out the culprits who stirred up the riots.

An official publication added that the central task of the Tibetan Buddhism Guidance Committee was to oversee the practice of Tibetan Buddhism in all of the Tibetan areas of the PRC.[118] (The placement of the Panchen Lama at the head of the committee was no doubt intended to increase the legitimacy of the unit.)

Tibetan Buddhism may well pose, in Tibetan areas, an ideological challenge to the orthodoxy upon which the political foundations of the PRC are based; and its nationalistic potential is clearly perceived by the authorities as posing a dire threat to the

---

[117] "Tibetan Leader Bainqen Interviewed," *Renmin Ribao*, September 28, 1988; in *FBIS*, September 29.

[118] Jing Wei, *100 Questions About Tibet*, p. 66.

legitimacy of Chinese rule in Tibet. However, respect for human rights, specifically the rights to freedom of expression and freedom of religion, requires that believers be allowed to organize and practice their faith as they wish, not as the state's rulers might want them to do.

In particular, the claim that Tibetan Buddhism, after centuries of existence without it, is now in need of a Chinese governmental bureaucratic unit in order "to help run well the monasteries according to religious doctrine,"[119] is hardly very convincing, and the same may be said of earlier official Chinese media pronouncements that monks who had taken part in demonstrations in Lhasa had been acting against their own religion.[120]

---

[119] Jing Wei, *100 Questions About Tibet*, p. 66.

[120] See for example "Events Described," an official commentary on the March 1988 demonstration in Lhasa: "A woman worshiper present on the occasion said 'These lamas are not at all like Sakyamuni's disciples, who show mercy to others'" (*Zhongguo Xinwen She*, March 5, 1988; in *FBIS* March 7, 1988). And according to "Tibetan Leaders Condemn Rioters," (*Beijing Review*, March 21-27, 1988): "[The Panchen Lama] told his listeners that the March 5 riot...went against the will of the Tibetan people and the teachings of Sakyamuni, founder of Buddhism." Following the imposition of martial law in Lhasa in March of this year, Phagpala Gelek Namgyal ('Phags-pa-lha Dge-legs rnam-rgyal), a high ranking Tibetan figure attending the Seventh National People's Congress in Beijing, told reporters that "The atrocities committed by the rioters [on] the previous occasions are a violation of the law and their religious teachings. Religious personalities have repeatedly admonished them. At present the religious circles are requesting the government to severely punish the rioters." (See "Tibetan Leaders Meet Press," *Beijing Television*, March 31, 1989; in *FBIS*, April 3.) More recently a ranking Tibetan Buddhist official said that "a small number of monks and nuns became involved in the riots in Lhasa in the past three years, creating

At the same time, it should be acknowledged that significant improvements have occurred in Tibet as regards freedom of religious expression in the period after 1979/1980. Tibetans are now able to engage in many of the outward manifestations of religious faith, while a number of monasteries and small temples have reopened, albeit with a greatly reduced cadre of active clergy compared to that found prior to the establishment of the PRC and with a severe limit on the extent of their activities. State funds have been used in the reconstruction of temples and monasteries (the great majority were damaged or destroyed prior to or during the Cultural Revolution), while donations in money and labor from Tibetans for this purpose have also been considerable. According to a recent official Chinese publication:

> Tibetan lamaists can hold various religious activities freely. They can set up shrines at home or create halls for chanting sutra and praying every day. They can also go to monasteries everywhere to worship and give alms. The observance of various religious holiday activities is also allowed.

> In downtown Lhasa, lamaists from different places can be seen kowtowing in front of the Jokhang Monastery. Inside halls are crowded with people adding butter oil to the burning lamps and bowing before Buddhist statues.[121]

---

social unrest and disrupting the normal order of production and the lives of the people. What they did...broke the Constitution and other laws and decrees, not to mention violating religious rules." ("Tibetan Official Views Monastery Management," *Xinhua*, September 29, 1989; in *FBIS*, October 3.)

[121] Jing Wei, *100 Questions About Tibet*, p. 60.

The limited leeway that religious expression has been given in Tibet in no sense permits the independent propagation of Buddhism or the unfettered management of religious institutions by Buddhist believers themselves. One Tibetan told Asia Watch that local Chinese cadres overseeing a monastery in the eastern part of the Tibetan Plateau had refused to permit the monks to perform nighttime rites in the surrounding hills. The cadres, coming upon the monks, had chased them back into the confines of the monastery.

When the Panchen Lama announced the creation of the Tibetan Buddhism Guidance Committee in the fall of 1988 he stated that it was meant in part to gradually change what he called the hard-line leftist practice of governmental intervention in religious affairs.[122] Since then, what are termed "democratic" administrative organizations are said to have been set up under the leadership of monks chosen by their respective monastic communities.[123] The Chinese government, however, has charged these management units with responsibility for guarding "against the influence of a small number of separatists,"[124] and the implication is that the new "democratic" management system, like much else in the structure of "regional autonomy" in Tibet, allots to local units the task of enforcing and implementing policies and directives from the Central Government. In such a context, these new units are clearly destined to function as further extensions of state power, thus merely reinforcing the suppression of the basic rights of Tibetans to free expression.

Since the implementation of martial law in the Lhasa region, all the previous long-standing mechanisms of

---

[122] "Tibetan Leader Bainqen Interviewed," *Renmin Ribao*, September 28, 1988; in *FBIS*, September 29.

[123] Jing Wei, *100 Questions About Tibet*, p. 62.

[124] "Tibetan Official Views Monastery Management," *Xinhua*, September 29, 1989; in *FBIS*, October 3, 1989.

governmental interference in religious affairs in Tibet - including restrictions on the free propagation and teaching of Buddhism, and the system of tight government control over monastic finances and over entry into the Buddhist clergy - have been further intensified. Any attempts from within the monastic community to extend its activities into the realm of dissenting politics is, as outlined earlier, rewarded by harsh and violent suppression and by political imprisonment or worse. We have no basis for assuming that the situation in the post-martial law period will change significantly.

8. Population Transfer

In *Human Rights in Tibet* we referred to several areas of human rights concern going beyond the questions of political imprisonment and the basic freedoms of speech, assembly and religion, namely those involving the imposition by the Chinese authorities of policies that are de facto socially discriminatory against the Tibetan population in Tibet. These policies relate to the continuing rapid growth of the Chinese population in Tibet; to birth control regulations for Tibetans; and education. The social disadvantages and inequalities flowing from these policies form, in Asia Watch's view, a contravention of the UN's *International Convention on the Elimination of All Forms of Racial Discrimination*, a covenant to which China acceded in 1981.[125]

The question of Chinese migration into Tibet remains a sensitive one. In our first report on Tibet we noted that the population figures given by Tibetan exiles for both Tibetans and Chinese on the Tibetan Plateau, 6 million and 7.5 million respectively, cannot be accepted. More recently at least some Tibetan exile officials have reduced that figure somewhat by taking it to include 1.2 million Tibetans who are said to have died as a result of China's annexation of the area of the TAR in 1951 and as a result of subsequent Chinese policies throughout the Tibetan Plateau; and by expanding its scope to include other nationalities living in Tibetan areas, some of whom, at least, may reasonably be considered to be Tibetan sub-groups.[126]

The official Chinese census of 1982 put the Tibetan population of the PRC at 3.87 million, and in January 1988 the Chinese Bureau of Statistics put the number of Tibetans at 4.74

---

[125] See *Human Rights in Tibet*, p. 72.

[126] See Tshe-ring dbang-phyug *Bod-kyi mi-'bor sa-ya drug skor lam-tsam dpyad-pa* (Dharamsala, 1989).

million, figures which Asia Watch broadly accepts.[127] (We should note that the last figure can only be an estimte as no new census has been taken). As regards the size of the Chinese population, the figure of 7.5 million for the number of Chinese in Tibet given by Tibetan exile authorities includes those living in areas such as **Xining**, the capital of **Qinghai** province.[128] This city has not been Tibetan for centuries and it lies outside the contiguous territory of Tibetan habitation formed by the various Tibetan and semi-Tibetan autonomous areas that occupy most of the Tibetan Plateau. Thus, this 7.5 million figure includes small stretches of territory on the eastern edge of the plateau that have a disproportionately high concentration of Chinese. While we still do not have an accurate figure for the number of Chinese on the Tibetan Plateau, it is undoubtedly below 7.5 million.

The Chinese authorities, on the other hand, for a long time insisted that there were only 73,000 Chinese in Tibet, a figure that would strike any visitor to Lhasa as being quite ludicrous. More recently, Chinese sources and official spokesmen commenting on the population of Tibet and Lhasa have provided certain statistics. Most strikingly, the vice-chairman of the TAR government, **Mao Rubai**, was quoted by an Indian wire-service dispatch as having stated that there were actually one million Chinese settlers in Tibet.[129] This figure has not been repeated by any other official source; indeed, since the imposition of martial law in Tibet, Chinese sources have again reverted to citing the earlier figure. In March 1989 an official news report stated, with regard to the TAR:

---

[127] Robert Delfs, "Mosaic of minorities," *The Far Eastern Economic Review*, August 25, 1988, p. 30.

[128] See Tshe-ring dbang-phyug, *Bod-kyi mi-'bor sa-ya drug skor lam-tsam dpyad-pa* (Dharamsala, 1989).

[129] "Chinese offer to Dalai Lama," *The Times of India*, September 27, 1988.

The population today is 2.07 million, of which around 2 million are Tibetan, accounting for 96 percent or more of the region's populace. Hans number some 70,000, mostly cadres, workers, and technicians from all parts of the country supporting Tibet's construction.[130]

Shortly afterward, another official report indirectly implied that there might, in fact, be a larger Chinese presence in Tibet than had previously been acknowledged. **Ngapo Ngawang Jigme** (Nga-phod Nga-dbang 'jigs-med), a prominent Tibetan member of the National People's Congress in Beijing and one of the most high-profile Tibetans in the Chinese government, was quoted as saying:

The Tibetan people cannot be separated from the support and assistance of the fraternal Han people. However, a large number of laborers, including peddlers and hawkers, have now flowed into Tibet, with a total of at least 100,000 in Lhasa alone. This has created a lot of trouble for public order.[131]

At first glance, this statement would appear to indicate that the peddlers and hawkers referred to by Ngapo were Chinese. In similar vein, an official broadcast describing a March 20 meeting of the Tibetan regional government commented:

In recent years there has been a big increase in the mobile population entering Tibet [i.e., implying that the floating population was made up of

---

[130] "Tibet Population Statistics Reported," *Zhongguo Tongxun She*, March 14, 1989; in *FBIS*, March 20.

[131] "'Radical Measures' Urged To End Riots," *Renmin Ribao*, March 23, 1989; in *FBIS*, March 24.

Chinese who had moved into the region from elsewhere in the PRC]. According to incomplete statistics there are as many as 30,000 to 40,000 of these people in Lhasa City alone. A considerable number of them have undergone the legal procedures and are engaged in industry, commerce, construction, catering services, and other operational activities. These activities have played an important role in invigorating the region's markets and its economy. This is the inevitable result of opening up to the world and developing the commodity economy.

At the same time, however, certain people have blindly flocked into Lhasa. This has had a serious impact on the city people's normal production, daily life, and work.

In order to learn about the situation regarding people who have come into the city from elsewhere, effectively strengthen security control, eliminate factors for instability, protect the legitimate rights of those who have come to the region to engage in lawful business, and ensure the healthy development of reforms and opening up, the regional government has decided that all people who have come into Lhasa from elsewhere must report for registration.[132]

A few days later the mayor of Lhasa, **Loga** (Blo-dga'), made comments to the effect that the excess population of the city was creating certain ethnic tensions. The mayor also noted, however, that the influx of people from the rural areas into Lhasa should

---

[132] "Tibet to Register All Outsiders in Lhasa," *Radio Lhasa*, March 20, 1989; in *FBIS*, March 21.

be strictly controlled. He placed the population of the city at 140,000, with a floating population of 100,000.[133] Shortly thereafter, a Chinese publication stated that there were over 3,000 people from "inland" areas (i.e., China proper) doing business in Lhasa and other Tibetan cities, along with about 400 Chinese craftsmen working on the streets of Lhasa.[134]

That the Chinese authorities are directing their population control efforts in Lhasa at Tibetans, rather than at Chinese settlers, has been made clear in other reports. **Dorje Tsering** (Rdo-rje tshe-ring), chairman of the regional Tibetan government was quoted by the Chinese press as stating that 40% of Lhasa's 100,000 people were transients from other Tibetan regions, and that those among them who were not contributing to Lhasa's economic development would be dealt with harshly.[135]

The massive Chinese presence in Lhasa (including itinerant peddlers, merchants, and others) is impossible to ignore. The official Chinese view that it is only the non-resident *Tibetan* populace of Lhasa (many, if not most, of whose members are transient pilgrims) that is at the root of social problems in the city is hardly very persuasive. Indeed, by putting forward population statistics that include only Tibetan "transients", the authorities seem purposely to be ignoring almost the entire Chinese population of the city. The majority of the population of Lhasa is clearly Chinese (as we noted in *Human Rights in Tibet*)[136] - a

---

[133] "Lhasa Mayor Views Progress, Problems in Tibet," *Radio Beijing*, March 27, 1989; in *FBIS*, March 30.

[134] Yang Xinhe, "Regional National Autonomy Spurs Tibet's Economic Development," *New China Quarterly*, May, 1989, p. 117.

[135] "Tibet Allots Riot Blame," *Newsday*, March 22, 1989; and "'Idle' transients told to leave Tibet," *The South China Morning Post*, March 22, 1989.

[136] *Human Rights in Tibet*, p. 43.

fact which doubtless accounts for the Chinese authorities' steadfast refusal to provide any reliable statistics for both Tibetans and Chinese in Lhasa.

In essence, the authorities appear to be applying a discriminatory policy aimed at barring Tibetans from coming to Lhasa, while placing no restrictions whatever on Chinese migration into the city. For example, housing in the Tibetan quarter of Lhasa is very badly maintained, and it continues to deteriorate, but the Chinese government has not hesitated to construct extensive new housing for the Chinese population.[137] And while admitting that housing in Lhasa is not in good shape and lacks amenities,[138] the authorities also imply that the need for better housing is but one more reason why "transients" (i.e. Tibetans) must be kept out of the city. Asia Watch believes that recent moves aimed at expelling Tibetans from Lhasa are unfairly designed to shape the ethnic and national make-up of the city in favor of the Chinese population. The formation of a professionally capable and strategically placed Chinese population seems to be the key element in the Chinese government's plans for the integrated economic and military development of Tibet - a goal pursued through sometimes romantic and idealistic appeals aimed at attracting ever-increasing numbers of Chinese settlers to Tibet.[139] The recent round of riots in the region has underscored the profound unwillingness of at least a significant portion of the Tibetan population to go along with such plans.

Asia Watch does not believe that the influx of Chinese into Tibet has meant that most parts of the region are swamped with newcomers. On the contrary, most of the TAR and the

---

[137] Ibid., p. 45-46.

[138] Luo Ga, "Lhasa: Growing Pains," *Beijing Review*, August 28-September 3, 1989; "Tibetan CPPCC Member on Reasons for Riots," *Zhongguo Xinwen She*, March 22, 1989; in *FBIS*, March 28.

[139] *Human Rights in Tibet*, p. 44-45.

neighboring Tibetan areas still remain almost exclusively Tibetan-inhabited areas. The Chinese population is concentrated in urban areas, and in places of strategic interest as regards security, communications, military, and other concerns. However, to say that most of the large tracts of nomadic grasslands or isolated agricultural areas have very few Chinese in them is hardly to say that the Chinese presence in Tibet is not problematic; such areas, especially in the western part of Tibet, also have relatively few Tibetans. The problems arise from Chinese settlement and domination of those places of greatest significance for the economic, social and cultural life of Tibetans. Chinese domination of those places threatens to marginalize much of Tibetan life and culture. Asia Watch is concerned at what appears to be a deliberate policy to accomplish such marginalization, as well as at the inherently discriminatory aspects of policies that are aimed at keeping non-resident Tibetans out of Lhasa while allowing non-resident Chinese the right to settle freely in the city.

9. Educational Discrimination

China's population policies in Tibet, particularly its encouragement of Chinese migration into the region, have generated inequalities that have put the Tibetan populace at a clear disadvantage. It is commonly known that the educational opportunities afforded Tibetans and Chinese in Tibet differ markedly, not least because of the language advantage Chinese have under the current system. Education beyond the elementary level generally requires a good knowledge of Chinese, since most of the instruction offered above that level is in Chinese. Chinese are also at a clear advantage in obtaining employment in positions linked to state-run enterprises, as they have the better language skills when it comes to taking requisite examinations that are generally in Chinese.

In recent years there has been some official recognition given to the lack of sufficient educational facilities in Tibet. In July 1988, **Li Tieying**, a member of the Communist Party Politburo noted the insufficiency of good schools, bilingual education, and trained teachers in Tibetan regions.[140] In December of that year the **Panchen Lama** commented that the study and development of the Tibetan language and of Tibetan Buddhism had become "a life and death problem" for Tibetans.[141] Previously the Panchen Lama had noted that resolutions aimed at strengthening the position of the Tibetan language in Tibet had been passed by Tibet's Regional People's Congress, but that no moves to implement them had ever been made.[142]

---

[140] "Li Tieying Discusses Promoting Tibetan Education," *Xinhua*, July 15, 1988; in *FBIS*, July 19.

[141] "Ngapoi, Bainqen Talk About Tibetan Studies," *Zhongguo Xinwen She*, December 6, 1988; in *FBIS*, December 12.

[142] *Evading Scrutiny*, pp. 15-16.

Official Chinese sources claimed in the fall of 1988 that 70% of school-age children in **Qinghai Province** were enrolled in schools.[143] Tibetans from the area cannot give specific figures for the number of schoolchildren, but they have noted that elementary education is reasonably widespread, and that in Tibetan areas it is usually carried out in the Tibetan language. This seems to be the case in the TAR too, and there appears to be an adequate number of elementary school textbooks available to Tibetans inside and outside the TAR. It is when one goes above the elementary school level that one finds an increasing decline in the status of the Tibetan language.

In late 1988 China published statistics dealing with the educational situation in the TAR in 1987, and listed 121,000 elementary school students out of which 90% or 109,000 were Tibetan; 22,000 middle school students, of whom 65.2% were Tibetan; 3060 vocational middle school students, of whom 69.6% were Tibetan; and three institutes of higher learning with 2860 students, of whom 66.4% were Tibetan. The same statistics also noted the presence of some 200 students in the region's Academy of Tibetan Buddhism and 5278 students scattered in middle schools in various provinces and regions of the PRC outside Tibet. The total number of students adds up to 154,398, but the same source also gave the "present" total (that is, as of late 1988) as 166,000, said to be 41.5% of the youth of the TAR.[144]

---

[143] Cheng Gang, "Qinghai Province's Tibetans," *Beijing Review*, October 17-23, 1988.

[144] "Xizang jianqi minzu jiaoyu tixi dazhongxiao xuesheng yiyu shiliu wan," *Renmin Ribao*, December 1, 1988. Most of the same figures for students in the TAR are given in Jing Wei, *100 Questions About Tibet*, pp. 42-43, but the percentage of school-age children in schools is given as 54.4%. A *Radio Lhasa* broadcast of April 21, 1989 gave the TAR's student population as being 165,000: "Editorial Cited on Tibet's 30th Reform Anniversary," *FBIS*, April 27, 1989.

The decline in the percentage of Tibetans among post-elementary school students in the TAR is clearly due to the decreased emphasis on the Tibetan language in middle and higher educational institutes. As one Tibetan student stated in January 1989 in an official Chinese publication, most middle school teachers in her area are from China proper; that is, they are non-Tibetans who undoubtedly cannot teach in Tibetan.[145] Similarly, **Punkang Tsering Dhondup** (Phun-khang Tshe-ring don-grub), a Tibetan member of the Chinese People's Political Consultative Conference, described the quality of teaching in Lhasa's schools as low. His solution was to call for more Chinese intellectuals to come to Tibet and work in the schools, regardless of the fact that this would constitute a further increase in China's dispatch of Chinese settlers into Tibet.[146]

That the authorities to some extent do acknowledge the inequities in this situation is implied in the promulgation in March 1989 of a set of *Regulations of the Tibet Autonomous Region on the Study, Use and Development of the Tibetan Language*. Official reports about the regulations noted, among other things:

> Schools in rural areas should concentrate on the Tibetan language, though standard Chinese is also required to be taught.

> Because of an inadequate supply of teaching materials and a shortage of teachers, the regulations pointed out the urgent need to make up this shortfall.

---

[145] Degyisangmo, "Tibetan Student in Beijing," *China Reconstructs*, January 1989.

[146] "Tibetan CPPCC Member on Reasons for Riots," *Zhongguo Xinwen She*, March 22, 1989; in *FBIS*, March 28.

By 1993 textbooks for middle schools should all be written in Tibetan; by 1997 most of the subjects in senior middle and technical schools should be taught in Tibetan; and after the year 2000, institutes of higher learning should gradually start to use the Tibetan language, the regulations state.[147]

These regulations were drawn up by the TAR government on the initiative, reportedly, of the **Panchen Lama** and **Ngapo Ngawang Jigme**. As we have already noted, the Panchen Lama had previously commented on the fact that earlier resolutions aimed at strengthening the position of the Tibetan language had received no more than lip service, so far as the actual situation in Tibet was concerned. Asia Watch's interest in this issue stems from the de facto discriminatory conditions that are produced when Tibetans are forced to compete for jobs and positions against native speakers of Chinese on the basis of their abilities in what is at best a second language for most of them. The awareness of the problem implied by the adoption of the regulations in question is laudable. But the extent to which they will be actually implemented, given China's previous track record on the issue and its adoption of harsher policies of control following the period of martial law, remains seriously in doubt. Although the regulations were announced after the proclamation of martial law and the riots that preceded it, they had obviously been prepared before that time, and undoubtedly reflect thinking that may now be considerably altered. More recently, high ranking officials in the TAR have begun to echo an older line linking the issue of access

---

[147] "Legislation Encourages Use of Tibetan Language," *Xinhua*, March 17, 1989; in *FBIS*, same date. See also "Law on Wider Use of Tibetan Language Promulgated," *Xinhua*, March 16, 1989; in *FBIS*, March 21.

to education at certain levels more tightly to political considerations. They assert, for example:

> We must settle the issue of what kind of people should be trained, and this issue carries a special and important significance in Tibet. We must train qualified personnel who love the motherland and maintain national unity, and by no means should we train people who seek to practice splittism. In weighing education in our region, we must see whether the students we train are politically qualified.[148]

The emphasis on Chinese as the language of instruction in Tibetan education and as the primary language for those aspiring to middle and higher level jobs in the TAR's infrastructure acts as an invisible but insuperable barrier to many Tibetans. The results of the Chinese-based educational system were described by a British teacher who went to Tibet as an English teacher at Tibet University in Lhasa from February 1987 to January 1988. She noted that the university's first class of English majors, which graduated in the summer of 1988, had been composed exclusively of Chinese students, the result of a system in which Tibetans must first master Chinese before they can study English (or most other subjects). Although she herself was part of an effort to ameliorate this situation, even in the work of that project resources meant for the advancement of Tibetan education were in fact diverted for the benefit of Chinese students.[149] More recently, the renewed emphasis upon "political qualifications" will undoubtedly cut opportunities even further. In short, Asia Watch considers current

---

[148] "Tibet Secretary Speaks at Education Forum," *Radio Lhasa*, September 11, 1989; in *FBIS*, September 14, .

[149] Julie Brittain, "Britain Bows to Chinese in Tibet Teacher Project," *The Hongkong Standard*, August 6, 1988.

educational conditions in the TAR to be biased against Tibetans, and to form part of a situation in which Tibetans are seriously threatened with marginalization within their own areas.

III. THE U.S. RESPONSE AND ASIA WATCH'S RECOMMENDATIONS

The response of the Administration to human rights abuses in the PRC on and since June 4, 1989 has been described in our recent report on China: *Punishment Season: Human Rights in China After Martial Law.*[150] In the aftermath of China's violent suppression of the pro-democracy movement in Beijing and elsewhere, it has become increasingly obvious to most observers that the Bush Administration, like the Reagan Administration before it, has placed a low priority on making the Chinese government's adherence to basic standards of respect for human rights an objective of US foreign policy. The failure of successive US administrations to acknowledge the severity of human rights violations in China as a whole applies also to the specific case of Tibet.

In October 1989, the Dalai Lama was present in the US when he was awarded the 1989 Nobel Peace Prize, but the Bush Administration, true to a policy that places a high priority on not offending the sensibilities of the Chinese government over Tibet, avoided all contact with the new Nobel laureate.

The US Congress, by contrast, has not hesitated to express its abhorrence at the continuing grave human rights violations in Tibet. Over the last three years Congress has adopted several strongly-worded resolutions expressing concern about Chinese governmental repression in Tibet[151] and calling upon the Chinese authorities to cease the repression. In 1989, the House and the Senate both passed resolutions condemning the imposition

---

[150] Published by Asia Watch, March 1990.

[151] These resolutions include the Amendment to HR 1777, December 22, 1987 (Foreign Relations Authorization Act); S Congressional Res. 129, September 16, 1988; Senate Resolution 82, March 15, 1989; House Resolution 63, May 16, 1989.

of martial law in the Lhasa area and continued human rights abuses in Tibet. A limited number of sanctions was formulated by the Bush Administration in June, but it included no reference to Tibet. However the sanctions bill that was passed by the Congress on January 30, 1990, included the following language on Tibet:

> (6) United States policy toward the People's Republic of China should be explicitly linked with the situation in Tibet, specifically as to whether --

> (A) martial law is lifted in Lhasa and other parts of Tibet:

> (B) Tibet is open to foreigners, including representatives of the international press and of international human rights organizations:

> (C) Tibetan political prisoners are released; and

> (D) the Government of the People's Republic of China is entering into negotiations with representatives of the Dalai Lama on a settlement of the Tibetan question...

Despite this legislation, human rights abuses in Tibet have not affected either the Reagan or the Bush Administration. From 1987, when China's leaders began publicly implementing the recent series of violent and repressive measures against Tibetan demonstrators, the U.S. continued to allow military supplies to go to China, even though evidence suggests that at least some have been used to support the implementation of repressive measures. Sikorsky helicopters were used by the PLA in overseeing operations against Tibetan demonstrators in the fall of 1987,[152] and were part of the support force for the PLA troops moved into the Lhasa area in March 1989.[153] The Administration also approved the sale of Boeing jets to China in spite of the fact that such aircraft have been used to ferry troops into Tibet. The airplanes in question were equipped with navigational technology that could allow them to be used for military purposes.[154] The sanctions bill passed by the Congress in response to the Tiananmen Square crackdown, banned all further sales of military equipment to China.

On a more positive note, the Administration's 1989 *Country Report on Human Rights Practices for 1989*, released in February, contained a detailed and condemnatory description of human rights practices in China and Tibet.[155] In documenting its assertion that "the human rights climate in China deteriorated dramatically in 1989," the report cited the continuing political imprisonment and torture of Tibetans in 1989.[156]

----

[152] Craig Covault, "Tibetan Flight Operations Face Challenges in Remote Regions," *Aviation Week & Space Technology*, October 12, 1987, p. 54.

[153] "170,000 Troops Deployed Near Lhasa," *The South China Morning Post*, March 8, 1989; in *FBIS*, same day.

[154] State department officials denied the equipment would have any important military value. *The New York Times*, July 8, 1989.

[155] Department of State, *Country Reports on Human Rights Practices for 1989* (Washington, D.C., 1990), pp. 802-825.

[156] Department of State, *Country Reports on Human Rights Practices for 1989* (Washington, D.C., 1990), p. 802. The report wrongly describes Tibetan Buddhism as currently "thriving" (albeit under tight controls). This clearly reflects the outsider's perception

Asia Watch believes that legislation and sanctions, by the US and other countries, aimed at curtailing human rights abuses in the PRC are apt and appropriate; such moves should treat human rights violations in Tibet as a central concern, and not as a side issue. Many of those who now realize that there are serious human rights problems in Tibet have come to this understanding only out of shock at the June 1989 violence in China; they tend to view conditions in Tibet simply in terms of their awareness of what is transpiring in China. It was this widespread reluctance to consider the situation in Tibet on its own terms that led many people (and most governments) to ignore or discount earlier instances of human rights violations in Tibet, when the visibility of such violations in the PRC as a whole was low.

In the current context, to allow the Chinese authorities to be brought back into the good graces of the international community (the obvious thrust of the Bush Administration's desire not to see China "isolated" on any account), on the basis of a possible amelioration of the situation outside of Tibet, would be a mistake. Moreover, systematic human rights violations cannot be quarantined within one part or region of a state's territory; inevitably, such abuses exert a corrupting influence throughout the society. Indeed, Tibet appears in retrospect as having been something of a testing ground for the PRC authorities in the 1980s, in terms of their experimentation and self-education in how best to forcefully suppress dissent and then deal with the international reaction.

A further international tendency has also been evident, namely, the downplaying of human rights violations in Tibet out of suspicion of or disagreement with the main objective of Tibetan

---

of external appearances, rather than being based upon the needs and perspectives of Tibetan Buddhist practitioners themselves. While it is true that there has been a considerable relaxation in restrictions on religion since the early 1980's, the natural vigor (intellectual and otherwise) of Tibetan Buddhism is still subject to serious checks and restraints.

protesters: the independence of Tibet. The Bush Administration has consistently reiterated its opposition to this objective - as have members of the Chinese pro-democracy movement. The absolute right of Tibetans to peacefully protest on this issue is guaranteed by provisions on freedom of expression and assembly in the Universal Declaration of Human Rights and other internationally recognized human rights covenants.

As this report makes clear, China's record in Tibet is in clear violation of accepted international norms of respect for human rights. Although the PRC condemns all criticism of its human rights record as unwarranted interference in its internal affairs, the PRC's accession to international instruments concerning human rights contradicts that position. Chinese actions and practices in Tibet, including discriminatory practices in furthering Chinese settlement in Tibet, arbitrary political arrests and imprisonment, restrictions on free speech and the use of torture, have placed the PRC in clear violation of the *Universal Declaration of Human Rights*, the *International Convention on the Elimination of All Forms of Racial Discrimination*, and the *Convention Against Torture and Other Cruel, Inhuman or Degrading Treatment or Punishment*. China has assumed an international responsibility to adhere to the standards set in these agreements, and is thus - despite its frequent protestations of "interference in China's internal affairs", "violations of sovereignty" and the like - directly accountable on these issues to the international community.

The PRC authorities insist that China fully adheres to human rights standards in Tibet, while at the same time refusing human rights workers access to the region. Asia Watch strongly urges that in addition to trying to secure Chinese adherence to minimal standards of human rights, the US should press the Chinese authorities for access to Tibet by independent human rights monitors so that they can directly observe conditions in Tibet. It is surely time that the PRC is put on notice that grave abuses will no longer be tolerated by the international community.

APPENDIX
Martial Law Regulations: Lhasa, March 1989

On March 7, 1989 the Chinese government issued three martial law decrees for Tibet, followed by three more the next day. All were signed by **Dorje Tsering** in his capacity as chairman of the regional Tibetan government. The texts of the martial law resolutions, are as follows:*157*

[Martial Law Decree 1:]

In accordance with the martial law issued by the State Council, the People's Government of the Tibet Autonomous Region has issued the following orders:

1. Start from zero hour of March 8, 1989, a martial law will be enforced in Lhasa city proper and in the area west of Lhamo [Lamo (La-mo)] Township, Dazi [Taktse (Stag-rtse)] County and east of Dongga [Dungkar (Dung-dkar)] Township, Duilong Deqing (Tolungdechen (Stod-lung bde-chen)] County

---

157 The texts of these decrees are copied verbatim, except for the emendation of place names in the first decree, from photocopies of the English-language versions of the decrees circulated by the authorities in Tibet. These copies are appended to the International Human Rights Law Group's "Communication to the United Nations Commission on Human Rights and Sub-Commission on Prevention of Discrimination and Protection of Minorities Concerning Human Rights Violations by the Government of the People's Republic of China," dated June 15, 1989. Cf the texts translated from broadcasts on Radio Lhasa in *FBIS* March 8 and 9, 1989.

2. During the time of the enforcement of the martial law, assemblies, demonstrations, strikes by workers, students and other people, petitions, and other get-togethers are strictly forbidden.

3. Traffic control measures will be implemented in the martial law enforced area. People and vehicles entering or going out of the area must go through formalities according to the regulations and receive security inspections.

4. Without permissions, foreigners are not allowed to enter the martial law enforced area. Foreigners who are now in the martial law enforced area must leave within a definite time, except those who have permissions.

5. Firearms and ammunition possessed illegally should be taken over. People who are not entrusted with the task of enforcing the martial law are not allowed to carry firearms and ammunition and other dangerous articles.

6. Public security organs and people entrusted with the task of enforcing the martial law have the right to search the riot-creating suspects and places where criminals are possibly hidden.

7. Those who resist to carry out the martial law and instigate others to do the same will be severely punished according to the law.

[Martial Law Decree 2:]

In order to safeguard the unity of the motherland, ensure the safety of citizens and personal property and protect public property from violation, the People's Government of the Tibet Autonomous Region specially issues the following orders:

1. It absolutely bans anyone in any case and in any form to instigate split of the country, create riots, group people to attack government offices, damage public property and undertake such sabotaging actions as fighting, smashing robbing, and arson etc.

2. Once the above-mentioned action happens, public security and police force and the P.L.A. men on patrol have the right to take necessary and strong measures to put the action down at once. Those who make above-mentioned action will be detained right on the spot, and if resistance occurs, police and armymen on duty can deal with them according to the law.

3. Any government institutions, units, mass organizations and citizens must immediately send criminals either found in operation or detected afterwards to judicial organs.

4. The judicial organs should make investigations of the crimes as soon as possible, handle cases without delay and give them heavy punishment in accordance with relevant decisions and articles of "The Decision of the Standing Committee of the National People's Congress on Heavy Punishment

to Criminals Who Seriously Violate Public Security"
and "Criminal Law."

[Martial Law Decree 3:]

In accordance with the martial law of the State
Council, the People's Government of the Tibet
Autonomous region has decided that traffic control
will be enforced during the time of martial law. It
specially issues the following orders:

1. All kinds of the motor-driven vehicles cannot
pass without the special permit or provisional passes
issued by the traffic police brigade of the Lhasa
Public Security Bureau. The persons who have the
provisional pass must go through the designated
way and within the fixed time.

2. Cadres, staff members must have identity cards
or certificates issued by their units; the officials and
soldiers of the People's Liberation Army and police
force must have armyman's permits; the officials
and soldiers of the public security departments
must have employees' cards or the identity cards on
patrol duty; students in schools must have their
student identity cards or their school's certificates;
those without jobs must have their resident identity
cards or their certificates issued by the house-hold
committees or relevant organs; those from out of
Lhasa must have temporary residence certificates;
monks and nuns must have the certificates issued
by the democratic management committees of their
monasteries; the preschool children should move
about with adults.

3. All kind of motor-driven vehicles on entering the martial law enforced area must show the certificates issued by the people's government of county level or above and apply for provisional passes; persons from out of Lhasa on entering the martial law enforced area must have certificates issued by the people's government of county level or above and must go through formalities for temporary residence within 5 hours after entering the area; cadres, workers and staff members of the Tibet Autonomous Region back from holidays and official business can enter the area with certificates which establish their identities.

4. Motor-driven vehicles and persons leaving the martial law enforced area must be approved by leaders of county level or above and have their unit's certificates.

5. Motor-driven vehicles and persons passing within the martial law enforced area or entering and going out of the area must receive security inspection by police and armyman.

6. If any persons violate the above-mentioned orders, the people on patrol duty have the right to examine them according to the different cases, adopt mandatory measures on the spot, and even look into responsibility for a crime.

[Martial Law Decree 4:]

In order to ensure the security of aliens in the martial law enforced area the People's Government of the Tibet Autonomous Region issues the following orders:

During the time of the enforcement of the martial law in Lhasa City, aliens cannot enter the area without permission. Aliens now in Lhasa must observe "martial law" issued by the State Council of the People's Republic of China and Orders of the People's Government of the Tibet Autonomous Region.

Foreign guests to Lhasa invited by the People's Government of the Tibet Autonomous Region and by other government organs must show "the Pass of the People's Republic of China" (which is called "Pass" for short below) issued by the Foreign Affairs Office of the People's Government of the Region when entering and going out of the area.

Foreign specialists and foreign staff members of joint ventures working in Lhasa must show "Pass" issued by public security authorities when entering and going out of the area.

Aliens who have obtained the right of residence in Lhasa must show valid residence identity cards when entering and going out of the area.

Foreign tourist groups organized by tourist agencies now staying in the Region can enter and go out of the area only if they are accompanied by Chinese guides with "Pass" issued by the public security authorities.

Unorganized foreign tourists now staying in Lhasa must leave in the time fixed by the public security authorities.

"The Pass" will be obtained at the Foreign Section of the Lhasa Public Security Bureau with "Residence Identity Card for Alien" issued by the public security authorities.

[Martial Law Decree 5:]

In order to fully reflect the policy of "leniency towards those who confess their crimes and severe punishment to those who refuse to do so, atone for a crime by good deeds and render outstanding service to receive rewards," and to resolutely crack down the separatists and those who have committed serious crimes of fighting, smashing, robbing, and arson, the People's Government of the Tibet Autonomous Region has issued the following orders:

Those who have plotted, created and participated in the riots, who have committed fighting, smashing, robbing and arson, and who have given shelters to criminals and booty, must surrender themselves to the police at once, so that they can receive leniency.

Those who know the facts of separatists' activities and crimes of fighting, smashing, robbing and arson, etc. should expose and report the cases to their units or to the public security authorities. These people should be protected. Those who retaliate against people who inform against them shall be severely punished.

[Martial Law Decree 6:]

All the people on patrol from the public securities, the police force and the People's Liberation Army must strictly keep discipline in order to fulfill every task under the martial law. The People's Government of the Tibet Autonomous Region issues the following orders:

1. Obey orders in all actions.

2. Stand fast at posts, and perform obligations faithfully.

3. Strengthen unity and cooperate closely.

4. Carry out policies firmly and patrol in a proper way.

5. Implement strictly "The Regulations for the use of Weapons and the Police Instruments by the People's Police."

6. Protect earnestly the public property and the life and the property of the people.